RELIGION IN LIFE CURRICULUM

Edited by Edward A. Fitzpatrick, Ph.D.

PRACTICAL PROBLEMS IN RELIGION

BOOK OF THE HOLY CHILD (Grade One)

LIFE OF MY SAVIOR (Grade Two)

LIFE OF THE SOUL (Grade Three)

BEFORE CHRIST CAME (Grade Four)

THE VINE AND THE BRANCHES (Grade Five)

THE MISSAL (Grade Six)

HIGHWAY TO GOD (Grades Seven and Eight)

Accompanying this Series is the RELIGION IN LIFE CURRICULUM for grades one to six and PRACTICAL PROBLEMS IN RELIGION for grades seven and eight.

Practical Problems in Religion

Prepared under the direction of

REV. RUDOLPH G. BANDAS, Ph.D., S.T.D. et M.

Professor of Dogmatic Theology and Catechetics
St. Paul Seminary

Diocesan Director of the Confraternity of
Christian Doctrine

ST. AUGUSTINE ACADEMY PRESS
HOMER GLEN, ILLINOIS

Nihil obstat:
  GEORGE J. ZISKOVSKY
  Censor deputatus

Imprimatur:
  ✤ JOHN G. MURRAY
  Archbishop of St. Paul

March 15, 1934

This book was originally published in 1934
by The Bruce Publishing Company.
This edition reprinted in 2017 by St. Augustine Academy Press
based on the original 1934 edition.

ISBN: 978-1-64051-044-9

INTRODUCTION

Though this book on the practical problems in religion is a part of the Religion in Life Curriculum, it may be used as an entirely independent book. It prints in full the questions relating to the religious life of today, and answers them in a sound theological manner. The questions themselves were originally selected from students in our schools. They are the actual problems which students themselves wanted answered, and which were found to exist in various places.

The history of this book is interesting. The *Highway to Heaven* series in its doctrinal text called the *Highway to God*, proposed these questions at the end of its respective chapters. The textbook was tried out in a number of classes, and the problems furnished the basis for very stimulating discussions. Many of the teachers felt it advisable that an authoritative answer by a competent theologian should be available to the teacher. We were very happy, indeed, to find so extraordinarily competent a priest as Father Bandas ready and willing to co-operate in this work of Catholic education. As a result of his co-operation, we make available these answers. As previously explained, they may be used independently or by the teacher who uses the *Highway to God* in her classes, or the priest who uses the book with converts, or in the instruction of non-Catholics preparing for marriage to a Catholic. The priest and the other teachers will find this a very valuable adjunct to his work. The page references in this book are to the *Highway to God* as a convenience for those who use the books together.

We shall naturally welcome any suggestions for the improvement of this book.

Edward A. Fitzpatrick

The Catechetical Institute,
Marquette University.

CONTENTS

PAGE

INTRODUCTION v

1. GOD THE CREATOR 1

2. THE STORY OF THE CREATION 2

3. ADAM AND EVE 3

4. WHY GOD MADE MAN 4

5. THE FIRST COMMANDMENT OF GOD 9

6. THE SECOND COMMANDMENT OF GOD 13

7. THE THIRD COMMANDMENT OF GOD 21

8. THE FOURTH COMMANDMENT OF GOD 24

9. THE FIFTH COMMANDMENT OF GOD 37

10. THE SIXTH AND NINTH COMMANDMENTS 42

11. THE SEVENTH AND TENTH COMMANDMENTS 47

12. THE EIGHTH COMMANDMENT 54

13. SIN 59

14. THE MESSIAH 65

15. PREPARE YE THE WAY OF THE LORD 67

16. THE EARLY LIFE OF CHRIST 72

17. THE DIVINITY OF CHRIST: THE MIRACLES 75

18. THE PUBLIC LIFE OF CHRIST: THE PARABLES . . . 79

19. Some Memorable Sayings of Christ 86

20. Christ and the Holy Eucharist 89

21. The Crucifixion 95

22. He is Risen 101

23. Mary, Full of Grace 105

24. Christ and the Apostles 110

25. The Holy Ghost on Pentecost 113

26. The Roman Catholic Church 114

27. Grace and the Sacraments 121

28. Baptism 127

29. The Confession of Sins 130

30. The Sacrament of the Holy Eucharist 133

31. Confirmation 139

32. Matrimony 142

33. Extreme Unction 145

34. Holy Orders 148

35. Prayer 151

36. The Commandments of the Church 157

37. The Saints 179

38. The Angels 184

39. The End of the Journey 189

1.

GOD THE CREATOR

Problem Questions, Chap. I, p. 7.

1. *What would you say to a boy if you heard him misuse the name of God?*

If you heard a boy misuse the name of God you should remind him that God Himself has forbidden us to do so. Such an act is a violation of the second commandment and therefore is sinful. Furthermore, it is only reasonable that we respect and reverence the name of God. He is our Creator and Father. He gave us life and provides for us during all the days of our life. Just as children respect their parents, so we, as children of the Heavenly Father, must always reverence and respect His name.

Again, a boy who begins to misuse the name of God should be warned of the danger of such a habit growing on him. It is easy to contract habits at such a time in his life. If these habits are not checked, there is danger of carrying them through life.

2. *What is the best reparation to God you can make when you hear someone using His name in vain?*

If you heard someone misuse the name of God, you could repeat to yourself one of the verses you have learned (p. 5): for example, "I will praise Thee, O Lord, with my whole heart." Again you could say that prayer you have heard so often: "Blessed be God, Blessed be His Holy Name." Also, if you think your correction will do any good, explain to the person why he should not use God's name in vain.

3. *A boy carelessly endangers his life and when warned says, "God is good, He will protect me." Do you think he is right?*

He is not right. God is good and He will protect us, but

1

anyone who without reason endangers his life, and expects God to protect him, is expecting too much from God. He commits a sin of presumption insofar as he hopes for extraordinary help from God. We are supposed to take the ordinary means of safeguarding and preserving our life. Our reason tells us as much. In addition we know that we ourselves are not masters of our own life. It belongs to God and we must use it as He wishes, since He is master both of life and death.

2.

THE STORY OF THE CREATION

Problem Questions, Chap. II, p. 13.

1. *What part should creatures play in your life? Can they help you to heaven? Can they hinder you?*

(The teacher will tell you what St. Ignatius of Loyola says in a great book he wrote, called the *Spiritual Exercises,* in answer to this question.)

Creatures are to be used insofar as they help us to work out our salvation.

They can help us to get to heaven. Since every created thing is a reflection of God's perfection, everything should in some way remind us of God. Again, the material things of this world sustain and aid us in the service of God. Finally, a proper disposition of earthly riches will convert them into heavenly treasures. (Cf. R. G. Bandas, *Catechetical Methods,* pp. 112–128.)

But these things can also hinder us from attaining our salvation. In fact, many people become so attached to them that they entirely lose sight of God and never think of the welfare of their souls. Some individuals, who have inherited great wealth or a large sum of money, become attached to it, and are as a result so engrossed in worldly pleasure that the thought of religion is far from them.

So important is this teaching that St. Ignatius makes it the foundation of all spiritual exercises. He writes: "And the other things on the face of the earth are created for man and that they may help him in prosecuting the end for which he is created. From this it follows that man is to use them as much as they help him on to his end, and ought to rid himself of them so far as they hinder him as to it." (*The Spiritual Exercises of St. Ignatius of Loyola,* translated from the autograph by Fr. Elder Mullan, S.J.)

2. *In what ways does the creation of the world reflect the greatness of God?*

The creation of the world reflects the greatness of God in the following ways:

In the first place, God had but to command and beings came into existence. He has power to make out of nothing. If we contrast the power of God with that of man, we shall understand that God's power is far superior to that of man. Man can do many things; for example, he has built airplanes, steamships; he has erected large cities throughout the land. These are indications of great intelligence and power, but what are they in comparison to all the things God has made by His Word only.

In the second place, consider the multitude of things created by God: from the tiniest creature visible only through the microscope, to the huge animals — what an assortment! The earth with its vegetative life and the heavens with their numerous planets are evidences of God's power and greatness.

Besides all this, when we begin to consider the perfect order among the various things of creation, we become more conscious of the great knowledge God possesses. Everything has its place and each fulfills its role, thus making for the general order in the whole world. No wonder the libraries of the world are filled with volumes that have been written in an attempt to describe God's creation. Men for thousands of years have been studying this wonderful work of God. To them it seems to be inexhaustible, so marvelous is the plan and order of the world.

3.

ADAM AND EVE

Problem Questions, Chap. III, p. 21.

1. *In the life of any saint, find out how he or she took care of her soul. Has this any suggestion for us?*

St. Thérèse of the Child Jesus.

The entire life of the Little Flower has been summed up by an eminent French writer in these few words: "St. Thérèse was a girl who loved her papa and mamma very much, and at the age of fifteen, entered the Carmelite Convent, where she died at the age of twenty-four." To the modern mind a life which can be so briefly sketched, seems to be insignificant and unimportant. She worked no miracles; she was never in the public eye; there was nothing remarkable about her life. On the contrary, she chose deliberately a "little way" so that we would realize that sanctity does not consist in great achievements but in ordinary things done well for the love of God. The routine of her daily work in the convent was much the same as the routine of any woman in the world caring for her home. Yet this ceaseless round of ordinary duties were the steps by which she reached heroic sanctity.

"There is a call," says Pope Pius XI, "to the faithful of every race, sex, and condition of life, to follow the little way of the Little Flower, which led St. Thérèse to the very summit of heroic virtue."

4.

WHY GOD MADE MAN

Problem Questions, Chap. IV, p. 26.

1. *Find in the New Testament any descriptions of life with God or heaven* (see Vaughn, *The Divine Treasury of Holy Scripture*).

"Be glad and rejoice, for your reward is very great in heaven.

For so they persecuted the prophets that were before you" (Matt. v. 12).

"Blessed are those servants whom the Lord, when He cometh, shall find watching. Amen I say to you, that He will gird Himself, and make them sit down to meat, and passing will minister unto them" (Luke xii. 37).

"And every one that liveth, and believeth in Me, shall not die for ever. Believest thou this?" (John xi. 26.)

"Let not your heart be troubled. You believe in God, believe also in Me. In My Father's house there are many mansions. If not, I would have told you, because I go to prepare a place for you" (John xiv. 1, 2).

"But, as it is written: That eye hath not seen, nor ear heard, neither hath it entered into the heart of man, what things God hath prepared for them that love Him" (I Cor. ii. 9).

"We see now through a glass in a dark manner; but then face to face. Now I know in part; but then I shall know even as I am known" (I Cor. xiii. 12).

"Unto an inheritance incorruptible, and undefiled, and that can not fade, reserved in heaven for you" (I Pet. i. 4).

"They shall no more hunger nor thirst, neither shall the sun fall on them, nor any heat" (Apoc. vii. 16).

"And I heard a voice from heaven, saying to me: Write: Blessed are the dead, who die in the Lord. From henceforth now, saith the Spirit, that they may rest from their labors; for their works follow them" (Apoc. xiv. 13).

"And God shall wipe away all tears from their eyes: and death shall be no more, nor mourning, nor crying, nor sorrow shall be any more, for the former things are passed away" (Apoc. xxi. 4).

"And there shall be no curse any more; but the throne of God and of the Lamb shall be in it, and his servants shall serve him" (Apoc. xxii. 3).

2. *Write a paragraph telling what you understand by the quotation from St. Augustine: "For Thyself, O God, Thou hast made us, and our hearts will not rest until they rest in Thee."*

St. Augustine means that no matter how much we may possess

in this world, we can never be fully satisfied until we are with God. We may have riches, and possessions; we may have health and the respect of our friends; we may have no temporal cares whatsoever, but yet there will always be a void in our lives, which these things cannot fill. In spite of our seemingly complete satisfaction there is something wanting, something missing from our lives. This is the story of everyman's life. St. Augustine himself is an example. As a young man God had no place in his life. In his middle age he thought to supply the need by immersing himself in the learning of his time, but all was fruitless. No wonder he could say and ardently, too, "For Thyself, O God, Thou hast made us, and our hearts will not rest until they rest in Thee." We find complete satisfaction in God, because He has created us for Himself and without Him we shall always be dissatisfied. He alone can fully satisfy all the cravings of our mind and heart.

3. *Show from the life of any saint, his or her love of God.*

The love of God played an important role in the life of St. Francis of Assisi. Although he was born of rather wealthy parents and although he himself took full advantage of being born into such circumstances, nevertheless, once he realized that God wanted him for a special work, without hesitation he gave up all. Unlike the young man in the Gospel he showed no desire to retain his possessions or his pleasures. He readily gave up all in order to serve God better. And this is no easy task. See how we cling to those things which give us pleasure and comfort. How greatly disturbed we are when we have to do without them even for a short time. How different it was with Francis. It was only because of his great love for God that he was able to forego honors, comforts, and pleasures.

And strange to say, Francis was more happy without any of the world's goods than when he was surrounded by them. Now he had time to think about God and the things of God and so great became his love of his Maker as the years passed that it embraced all the creatures of God. His love of things of nature which show forth the goodness and splendor of God, is well known. All the creatures of earth had a place in his all-embracing love of God. Man, the greatest of God's creatures on earth, was the special object of His love. The greater part of his life he devoted to working for man's welfare. By his good example, by his preaching and teaching, he labored to bring his fellow men nearer to God and to set them free from their vices and passions. In this work his only motive was the love of God. He loved man as God's creature; and the same was true of his attitude toward nature as a whole.

Here we can learn a very salutary lesson. Some may think that love of God makes one center all his attention on himself; instead, it liberates us from ourselves and makes us kindly toward all. It includes above all a great reverence for our Maker and His commandments, and brings all the rest of His creation into our scheme of life.

4. *Show from the life of any person not a saint his or her love of God (e.g., Lincoln).*

In the life story of Joyce Kilmer there are many incidents illustrating his great love of God. A convert to Catholicism, he said he obtained faith by prayer and hoped to obtain love of God in the same way. He writes in one of his letters: "Pray that I may love God more. It seems to me that if I can love God more passionately, more constantly, without distraction, that nothing else can matter." "I got faith by praying for it. I hope to get love the same way." Again in another letter he writes: "Pray for me, my dear Father, that I may love God more and that I may be unceasingly conscious of Him — that is the greatest desire I have."

Apparently the predominating desire of his whole life was to increase and grow in the love of God. His poems are evidences of this. Almost every one of them gives expression to religious thought or sentiment — a fact which can only be explained by his deep consciousness of the place God must have in our lives.

Another fact that brings out his longing for the love of God is his daily reception of Holy Communion. After his conversion and even when in active service during the war he always made it a point to receive Communion as often as possible. "Except while we are in the trenches, I receive Holy Communion every morning, so it ought to be all the easier for me to attain this object of my prayers." The object he refers to is Love of God. The labor of his life was to possess and increase in himself love for his Maker.

Biographical note:

Joyce Kilmer was born in New Brunswick, New Jersey, on December 6, 1886. In his youth and until 1913 he remained attached to the religion of his parents. In 1913 he became a Catholic. Most of his years after graduation from Columbia in 1906 were devoted to writing for various Reviews and newspapers. He also traveled extensively on lecture tours. In 1917 he enlisted in the army and left for France the same year. On July 30, 1918, he was killed in action.

5.

THE FIRST COMMANDMENT OF GOD

Problem Questions, Chap. VI, pp. 48, 49.

1. *You find a poor man alone in a hut. He is very ill and you advise him to make his peace with God. He tells you that his sins are too great to be forgiven. What sin does he commit by entertaining such thoughts? What would you tell him? Could you give him an example of great sinners who were forgiven by God because they repented sincerely?*

He commits a sin of despair.

God is merciful and is always willing to pardon even our greatest sins. In the Bible we read, "If your sins be as scarlet, they shall be made white as snow." The greatness of the sin should never deter us from sincerely and sorrowfully confessing it.

The penitent thief is an outstanding example. Though he led a sinful life, one request for help from the Savior won him entrance into eternal happiness.

Mary Magdalen was a sinner who, because of her confidence and trust in the mercy of God, was forgiven much.

St. Augustine likewise was a notorious sinner; he was converted, and finally became a great defender of the Faith.

2. *Your parents attend a funeral service at a Protestant church and wish you to go along. May Catholics attend such services? Would they be allowed to attend any Protestant services? Catholics are eager to have Protestants come to their church; why should they not return the courtesy?*

Catholics may go to such services provided they do not take any active part in these services.

9

No. They are not allowed to attend any and every Protestant service.

Catholics are eager to have Protestants come to their Church because they know that their Church is the true one, and at the same time hope that these non-Catholics may eventually belong to that Church. Their eagerness to have them come to the Catholic Church is an indication of their desire to bring the light of the true Church to those who are not privileged to be its members.

They cannot return the courtesy because they know that to attend Protestant services is practically a denial of the true faith and an approval of a false religion.

3. *A young man is leading a very sinful life. He realizes that he should change his ways and make his peace with God, but he always tells himself that there will be time enough tomorrow. What sin does he commit?*

He commits a sin of presumption.

4. *Mary is in serious trouble and becomes discouraged. She wishes that she would die. May she entertain such a wish? May people ever wish to die? Under what circumstances?*

She may not entertain such a wish. People may entertain such a wish only when they are motivated by the desire to be with God in heaven. In all instances when we pray for death, we must make our petition conditional upon God's will and good pleasure. Troubles and hardships are part of our lot in this life and are valuable aids in helping us to win greater reward in the next life.

5. *Henry and George are walking along the street when they suddenly meet a gang of rough boys. The boys stop them and ask them whether they are Catholics. Must the two tell them? What is the reason for your answer?*

They must admit that they are Catholics, since these rough boys may already be aware of the fact that the two are Catholics. In that instance, if the two boys denied that they were Catholics, they would be branded as liars and would bring harm to their religion.

6. *Sue and Jane go to the fortune teller "just for fun!" The fortune teller tells Sue something which really comes to pass shortly afterwards. Sue asks you what you think about it. What would you tell her?*

In the first place Sue should be told that no fortune teller possesses the gift of prophecy. Man cannot know anything that does not come within the domain of one or several of the five senses. Future events belong to this class. Hence, no fortune teller can predict anything of the future. If something comes to pass, it can be attributed to coincidence or human ingenuity. Further, Sue should be told to discontinue consulting such individuals. Such a practice is a danger to the faith.

7. *Jack never went to any other but a good Catholic school. He seemed to be a good boy, but shortly after he went to work he lost his faith. What, do you think, might have been the cause?*

The cause of Jack's loss of faith may be attributed to his failure to attend to his religious duties; for example, failure to attend Mass on Sundays, failure to receive the sacraments regularly, failure to recite his daily prayers. It may also be caused by evil companions whose bad influence has led him to contract evil habits.

8. *Someone sends you a chain prayer and tells you that you will be visited by some terrible calamity if you do not say it and help to circulate it. What should you do about it? What sin do you commit by believing in such things? Mention other superstitions you know about.*

You should disregard it entirely. By believing in such things you commit a sin against faith, because you desire to have your own wish fulfilled independently of the will of God.

Other superstitions are: (*a*) Belief in divination and dreams. (*b*) Such things as: belief in obtaining good luck through possession of a horseshoe; expecting bad luck because you saw a certain cat; belief that bad luck will come to you on Friday, on the thirteenth, etc.

9. *You have a rosary that was blessed by the Holy Father. It is valued at 50 cents, but a friend offers you $5 on account of the blessings it bears. May you accept the money for the rosary? May you accept any money? May you give it to your friend as a gift?*

No. You may not accept the money, because he evidently believes he is paying for the blessing. It would be simony to accept money in such a case.

You may accept money for the rosary provided you or the one who gives the money does not consider it as a price paid for the special blessing on the rosary.

You may give it to your friend as a gift.

10. *Louis wears a four-leaved clover for good luck. You laugh at him, but he says you are just as bad, for you wear a medal and believe it is going to keep away all harm. How will you explain the difference?*

The medal has a blessing attached to it and it is worn as an expression of devotion and confidence in the person whom it represents. Every time we look at a medal we are filled with good thoughts and are moved to prayer; it is because of these pious sentiments that God blesses us. A four-leaved clover has no blessing attached to it and is an indication of a superstitious belief.

11. *A thief steals some money from church. Later he repents. In confessing his thefts, must he make any distinction between what he took from the church and what he stole elsewhere? Suppose the money he took from church amounted to very little? What do we call such a sin? What other sins are called sacrileges?*

The thief when confessing should make a distinction, because the fact that he stole from a church is a circumstance which affects the nature of the sin.

Although the amount taken might be very small, still it would be a sacrilege. However, it would not be as great a sin as if he had stolen a great amount.

Other sacrileges are:

a) Unworthy reception of any of the sacraments.

b) Malicious striking of one in holy orders.

c) The destruction or theft of things dedicated to religious use.

12. *John's mother advises him not to go with certain companions because they are harmful to him. He tells her not to worry, for he knows how to take care of himself and will not follow their bad example. Is John right?*

John is not right. Even though he does not intend to follow their example, nevertheless they are an occasion of sin for him, and "whosoever loves the danger shall perish therein."

6.

THE SECOND COMMANDMENT OF GOD

Problem Questions, Chap. VII, pp. 55–57.

1. *During the day, so often, children, you think of your parents, your home, the baseball game. How often do you think of Jesus? Your mother loves you when you say, "Mother, dear," and such loving words sincerely. Wouldn't Jesus love you much, too, if during the day you would often say to Him, "Jesus, Jesus"? How often do you think you could easily do so? Try it this day at every change of lessons.*

Let the teacher read the problem slowly and let the child make a silent examination of conscience.

2. *How could you show reverence to the holy name of Jesus?*

By bowing my head and taking off my hat when hearing the Holy Name pronounced, by never using His Name in vain, by saying the Litany of the Holy Name, by thinking of what the Name of Jesus means to us (Savior), by correcting others when they use His Name in vain, by reciting with great fervor the Divine Praise after Benediction, by beginning every task in the Name of the Lord, by invoking the Holy Name in temptations.

3. *What do you think of a child who laughs upon hearing another child say the name of God in an angry or irreverential tone? Which child, do you think, has committed the graver sin?*

The child who laughs at the other is probably committing the greater sin because he thereby approves of the words of the first child and adds some malice of his own; namely, taking pleasure in hearing another sin. A child who laughs upon hearing another child say the name of God in an angry or irreverential tone minimizes the seriousness of the other's sin and thereby gives scandal.

4. *You are a young boy. You hear one of the big boys using very bad language and often saying the Holy Names in a shocking way. Would you let him talk like that, or would you have courage enough to tell him not to speak so? Tell the class what you would really say to him.*

I would tell him that he is misusing the tongue that God gave him; he should use his tongue to praise God rather than to pronounce His Name disrespectfully. His tongue was the first member of the body which the priest in baptism consecrated to God by placing blessed salt upon it; a boy who swears contradicts his morning prayer, "Hallowed be Thy Name"; he desecrates the tongue which was consecrated by the Body and Blood of Christ in Holy Communion; he is misusing the Name of Him who created him, redeemed him, sanctified him, daily blesses him, and who one day will stand before him as Judge; it is the one and only Name he will wish to invoke at the moment of death. Blaspheming and cursing is the language of the demons and souls damned in hell. A name expresses personality; by dishonoring the Divine Name we dishonor the Divine Person.

5. *How would you make good the wrong you have done by using the name of God in anger before a group of children?*

I would go to confession. I would also make a public apology. I would show great respect in the future for the Holy Name before the same children when the opportunities present themselves.

6. *The priest has given the order that the next one he hears cursing on the playground will be expelled. You hear a boy, who always used bad language when no teacher or priest is near, do so. What would you do or say to him?*

Tell the boy that although he may fool the priest or teacher by cursing in their absence, he cannot fool God who sees and hears everything. Tell him that the penalty of expulsion is as nothing compared to the punishment which the all-knowing Judge will one day mete out to those who misuse and abuse His Name.

7. *A boy thinks it is smart to imitate the bad language he hears from grown-up people. He shows off before his friends through cursing. What kind of sin do you think he is committing and how many?*

Sin of cursing, bad example, scandal, vanity.

8. *Why should such expressions as "Cross my heart, I'm telling the truth," and "Sure as heaven," even though they are not sins, very seldom be used?*

Such expressions should not be used because they are the beginning of a habit of making oaths carelessly and rashly.

9. *What is the best act of reparation to God you make when you hear someone using His name in vain?*

Pronounce the Holy Name devoutly; make an act of sorrow to God for the person you hear using His Name in vain.

10. *How could a group of boys prevent one or more boys from using the Holy Names profanely or from using vulgar expressions on the playground, without telling the teacher on them?*

By insisting on the omnipresence and omniscience of God, by telling them just what the Holy Name means to us, by excluding them from their games, hikes, parties, etc. (Cf. answer to No. 4.)

11. *A little boy or girl has come to school with the evil habit we are discussing. The parents thought it "cute" when the little one would use these words. How could the children at school help the child to break this habit without offending the parents?*

The children at the school should show the child why it is wrong to use such language. They should explain the Second Commandment. (Cf. answer to No. 4.)

12. *How would you act toward a child who is trying to overcome his vicious habit, but who very often does forget himself?*

Act kindly toward such a child and encourage him in his attempts to overcome such a vicious habit. Tell him to pray hard, especially in the morning at the beginning of the day. You should also pray for him, asking God to help him.

13. *Should your father at times say very unbecoming and even sinful words, could you tell him it is wrong and you do not like it? If he gets angry with you for telling him could you show him some other way that you don't want him to talk like that?*

Certainly, tell him that such words are sinful and wrong. If he gets angry with you for telling him, let no opportunity pass without showing the proper attitude in this regard. Use the Holy Name reverently. Pray for him. Leave the room when he uses such language; leave a group where such language is heard; shun people who use similar language.

14. *I know of a certain child who was purposely taught to curse by another person. The parents are much grieved, but again and again the child will forget himself. What do you think of the guilt of the person who is responsible?*

The guilt of the person who is responsible is very great. His guilt is proportionate to his bad intention. Such a person is unusually malicious. He does not understand how great is God's love for His creatures.

15. *A little boy has followed the example of his father in cursing. When the mother corrects him, he says: "Daddy does it, why can't I?" What do you think that mother ought to do?*

The mother should first correct the father. Then she should have the father explain to the boy that such language is sinful and wrong. If the father refuses to stop his cursing and also refuses to tell the boy, the mother should correct the boy. She should keep him out of hearing range if possible when the father curses.

16. *Some men so readily curse their horses, or cars, or what not. What do you think of such ingratitude to God?*

Such ingratitude flows from their poor understanding of the truth that God created all things; that He gave them to us as gifts to be used, not for the injuring of the soul, but as helps (aids) in our journey toward eternity.

17. *What can you do in your own families, even though you are quite young, and even though your family never uses coarse and sinful language, to raise its moral standard still higher in reference to the Second Commandment?*

Try to understand fully not only what the commandment forbids but also what it positively commands.

18. *What do you think a good Catholic young person would do, should he find that his friends, time and again, use profane language or speak deridingly of holy things?*

He will see to it that such "friends" cease using profane language and show respect for holy things. If they refuse, he will have nothing more to do with these "friends," because they are not true friends if they do not respect things which he considers as sacred and holy.

19. *Some young men commonly indulge in (as one writer puts it) "deviled" language. They frequently use words that refer to hell, Satan; this is often called "swearing," but it is only vulgar. Although these words in themselves are not sinful, what about the scandal given to bystanders and especially to children?*

Such language may do untold harm in the long run, especially to children who do not distinguish between this kind of language and real swearing; it may be the beginning for them of a bad habit of swearing and use of abusive language. Secondly, such language scandalizes the outsiders and those who consider it as swearing.

20. Very often Catholics themselves, by their free and jocose way of speaking, are the cause of others deriding religion. What should these Catholics do to overcome their habit?

Such Catholics should control their tongues better and be careful of their speech in the future. They should cultivate henceforth the habit of speaking in a serious manner about religion, thereby giving good example, and correcting the bad impression which they made previously.

21. What do you think of a magazine which will permit cartoons that put some one or other teaching of the Church or some member of the clergy, perhaps the Pope, in a ridiculous light? If you are subscribing to such a magazine and in general it is a good paper, what will you do?

Write to the editor or to those who have charge of the printing of the magazine and protest against the cartoons in question. Give the reasons for your protest. If the protest is of no avail, cancel your subscription.

22. What do you think of the Holy Name Society?

The Holy Name Society is doing much to further knowledge and respect for the Holy Name of God and of His Divine Son, and is powerful to raise the moral standard of the people. From the promises which its members make we learn that each member works individually for God's glory, for the spread of the Kingdom of God among those who do not know or who despise the Holy Name. The members further promise that they will never use the Holy Name irreverently, that they will avoid all indecent and profane language, false and unnecessary oaths, and blasphemy; that they will do all they can to teach others to have the highest respect for God's Holy Name. They promise always to fulfill their religious duties, and in most places they go to Holy Communion in a body at least once a month. They also pray for deceased members and carry on many other works for the welfare of the Church and the glóry of the Holy Name.

23. Why are such expressions as "God is cruel, unjust"; "God doesn't care for me"; "What good is praying anyway?" etc., in time of trial or sorrow, so grievously sinful?

Such expressions are blasphemous and untrue. They show a lack of faith in the providence, goodness, and omniscience of God who alone knows what is best for us.

24. If any expressions like the above are made without due deliberation, and the person is immediately sorry, what do you think of the sin?

They are perhaps only venial sins.

25. You are called upon the witness stand. Your own good name will be tarnished and perhaps your money lost if you tell the whole truth about the defendant, who is your business partner, your relative, or your friend. You have sworn "To tell the truth, the whole truth, and nothing but the truth; so help me God!" Regardless of your loss, what must you do?

One must tell the whole truth; otherwise it would be perjury and a very serious sin.

26. On the witness stand you have become all muddled in a cross-examination. You tell an untruth. Have you committed perjury?

If you have not told the untruth with deliberation and premeditation, you have not committed perjury. Such a thing could happen to the most honest man when he becomes muddled and excited.

27. A man swears never to forgive his wayward son or daughter. What do you know about such an oath?

Such an oath is rash. It is a serious sin against charity.

28. Why does the Church forbid secret societies like the Freemasons?

The Church forbids secret societies such as the Freemasons because such societies have in the past, and in certain countries, required oaths of their members which were against religion. They have been anti-Catholic and anti-religious. A lodge with many tends to take the place of the Church. Many of the leaders have however in certain parts of the United States been very strongly opposed to the Catholic Church and to the parochial school. It is a precept of the Church not to join the Freemasons because of the dangers to faith.[1]

29. *Such expressions as "God knows," "God is my witness," "Before God," can be oaths or not. What does this depend upon? (Intention of both parties.) Why should you avoid such strong language as "I swear," or "Upon my soul!" even though they do not mean an oath?*

Even though such expressions do not imply an oath, they should be avoided because they may lead to the taking of unnecessary oaths, or they may give scandal.

30. *A girl twelve years old became mortally sick. She promised to consecrate her life to God should she recover. This was some years ago. She recovered but has not kept her promise. What have you to say about this?*

The girl was probably in such poor physical condition that she was not able to deliberate sufficiently before making such a promise. Again, she was probably not old enough to know the implications of her promise. Perhaps it has not yet been possible for her to do what she promised God she would do. She is probably not bound to keep the promise. She should consult her confessor.

---

[1]Gasparri's *The Catholic Catechism*, p. 131, Question 242.

7.

THE THIRD COMMANDMENT OF GOD

Problem Questions, Chap. VIII, pp. 67–69.

1. *Grandmother is very ill and cannot be left alone. You are asked to remain at home with her while the rest go to Sunday's Mass. May you do so if there is no other Mass? What reason can you give for your answer?*

Since your grandmother is so ill that she cannot be left alone, you may remain away from Mass to take care of her. Under such circumstances you are excused from attending Mass. You are still honoring God by doing a necessary good to one of His creatures.

2. *Your father takes you on a fishing trip early Sunday morning. You plan on stopping at the next town to hear Mass, but by the time you get there Mass is over. Are you excused?*

If you tried to ascertain beforehand at what time Mass is said at the next town, and if you started out sufficiently early in the morning to get there in time, and if then for some unforeseen reason you were delayed on the way, you would be excused if you arrived late. Otherwise you should have attended Mass before leaving.

3. *A railroad man has to work on Sundays and cannot hear Mass. May he keep his job? Every few weeks he gets off Sunday mornings just at the time when Mass is half over. He reasons that as long as he could not get a whole Mass there is no need of his going to church. Is he right?*

Yes, a railroad man may keep his job and miss Mass if he would lose his job by attending Mass. He would lose his means of making a living for himself and family. Thereby he would suffer grave temporal loss. However, he may not reason that as long as he cannot get to a whole Mass he will not go at all. He who cannot attend the whole Mass is nevertheless bound to assist at the consecration and communion, if he can. He can possibly supply the omitted parts by assisting at the next Mass.

4. *A young man is out all Saturday night. Before returning home on Sunday morning he enters church to hear Mass. He sleeps during the greater part of the service. Has he fulfilled his obligation? What must one do in order to fulfill the obligation of hearing Mass on Sundays?*

The young man has not fulfilled the obligation of hearing Mass on Sunday since he did not advert to what was going on at the altar during the consecration and communion (which parts constitute the greater and essential parts of the Mass). If he slept only a little during the Mass, he fulfilled the obligation. But in this case as stated, the young man slept soundly for the greater part of the Mass. "They who sleep a little satisfy the precept, as long as they advert to the principal parts of the Mass."[1] He was physically and morally present but he did not assist with the proper attention. In order to fulfill the obligation of hearing Mass on Sundays, one must be present physically (bodily), morally (i.e., not separated from the altar by too great a space), continually (i.e., from the beginning to the end of Mass, at least from the beginning of consecration through the communion), and religiously (i.e., with attention of mind and intention of honoring God).

5. *A group of boys plan to go camping for three weeks. Fred is sent to select the place and the boys remind him that he must make sure that they will be able to hear Mass on Sundays. Fred returns and says that there is a Catholic church two miles distant. When they arrive, they find that this is not a Catholic church and that there is none near by. Suppose Fred knew all the time that this was not a Catholic church, how much of the blame must he take upon himself? Would it be enough for him to confess that he missed a Sunday's Mass? Suppose he really thought he was right, would the matter be different? Should the boys remain at the camp?*

If Fred knew all the time that this was not a Catholic church or that there was none near by, he is certainly to blame both for his and for the others' missing Mass. It would not be enough for

---

[1] A. Tanquerey, *Synopsis Theologiae Moralis* (Tournai, Desclee, 1927), Vol II, p. 682.

him to confess that he missed a Sunday's Mass; he must also confess that he was to blame for the others having missed Mass. If Fred really thought he was right, he and the others would be excused from hearing Mass the first Sunday. The boys should not remain at such a camp. There are plenty of good camps and camp sites which are near Catholic churches. They should select one of these.

6. *A working girl receives the news that her mother is very ill and she is needed at home. It is Sunday, and in order to be ready for the journey, she will have to do some laundering and sewing. May she do so?*

She may do her laundering and sewing in such a case because of the fact that a higher work of mercy demands that she should go on such a journey. Such work is necessary in this case and is therefore allowed.

7. *Six girls are invited out to a camp for a week-end. They know there is no Catholic church in the vicinity. Several of the girls say that since it is impossible for them to attend Mass they are excused. Are they right?*

Those girls who say that they are excused from attending Mass for such a reason are wrong and commit sin if they do not attend Mass. The Sunday (attendance at Mass) comes first, pleasure and recreation afterward.

8. *You are on your way to Mass on Sunday. A car ahead of yours is turned over and the driver is injured. If you stop to help him you will miss the only Mass there is at your church. Should you offer your help or go to Mass?*

Offer to help the injured driver. One would have a strict obligation in charity to help such a person. To refuse help may mean the driver's death, both physical and spiritual. "But he said to them, What man shall there be among you, that hath one sheep: and if the same fall into a pit on the Sabbath day, will he not take hold on it and lift it up? How much better is a man than a sheep? Therefore it is lawful to do a good deed on the Sabbath days" (Matt. xii. 11–12).

9. *Since Mr. Grey owns a radio he does not go to Mass on Sundays. He says he hears Mass and a good sermon every Sunday over the radio and really gets more out of it than when he goes to church. Is he in the right?*

Mr. Grey is wrong in his opinion. To fulfill one's obligation of hearing Mass on Sundays, one must be physically and morally present (cf. answer No. 4 above). Physical presence means to be at Mass in person; moral presence implies some connection between the person and the altar. Hearing Mass over the radio does not constitute physical and moral presence.

10. *Jack stays home from Mass on Sunday in order to shovel snow. He says the janitor shovels snow in front of church and if he has a right to do so, so have other people. What will you tell Jack?*

The janitor shovels snow on Sunday because it is necessary and allowable in his case; one of his duties is to keep the walks clear to allow access to the church. Mothers, nurses, custodians (janitors), soldiers on duty, and others who have necessary duties to perform, and cannot get to Mass on account of these duties, are excused from attending Mass on Sundays. Besides, the janitor goes to Mass either before or after shoveling the snow, or he shovels the snow before Mass begins. Jack is not excused from hearing Mass in such a case because it is not necessary for him to shovel snow during the Mass.

11. *A farmer and his family were just ready to start for Mass on Sunday morning when they noticed that a heavy storm was threatening. In order to save his crops the farmer went out into the field and also ordered his hired men to do the same. They all missed Mass. Were they justified in doing so? Give reason for your answer.*

Yes, the farmer, his family, and his hired help are all justified in this case in missing Mass, because the farmer's livelihood depends on his crops. It is a case of urgent necessity. The natural law of self-preservation comes before the ecclesiastical law of attending Mass on Sundays. The farmer's obligation to feed and support his family is greater than his obligation to attend Mass.

He must have help to save his crops; hence the hired men and his family were also excused from hearing Mass.

12. *Don wanted to paint the garden fence on Sunday afternoon, but his father would not permit him to do so, as that is servile work and therefore sinful. Don says that their neighbor paints pictures every Sunday and says that it is no sin. Is there any difference?*

There is a difference. Painting a fence is a servile work, a work of labor, and is forbidden by the Third Commandment. Painting pictures is a work of skill and a product of the brain, a work of art. Such is not forbidden.

13. *Mary and Jane live on a farm. They have to remain home from Mass every other Sunday to take care of the children and the house. Mother tells them they ought to recite the Mass prayers at home, but Mary says that will do no good as long as they cannot attend Mass. What do you think about the practice?*

To recite the Mass prayers in such a case — though not an obligation — is a laudable practice and should be encouraged. The girls are excused from Mass; but they should try in some other special way to pray to God and worship Him on Sundays. There is a certain family at Bloomfield, Montana, living thirty miles from the nearest church. They recite the Mass prayers in common every Sunday and holyday on which they cannot attend Mass.

14. *Mr. Daly goes to a low Mass every Sunday and then goes out fishing or hunting. Mr. Smith, his neighbor, tells him that hearing a Mass is not enough to "keep holy the Sabbath." If you were Mr. Smith, how would you explain the case to Mr. Daly?*

If this is Mr. Daly's only form of recreation during the week, he may go fishing or hunting on Sunday as long as he attends Mass devoutly whenever he is required to do so. Hunting and fishing for pleasure do not constitute servile work. However, Mr. Daly should also attend other religious functions, if there are any, on Sunday in order to keep in mind that the day belongs to God. Legitimate recreation is allowed on Sunday.

15. *"You are not keeping the word of God," says a non-Catholic to you. "The Bible says, 'Remember thou keep holy the Sabbath day,' and you Catholics keep Sunday instead." Is there a difference between Sabbath and Sunday? How would you explain the position of Catholics?*

The word *Sabbath* means a day of rest. The Sabbath of the Old Law was the seventh day of the week; our Sabbath, or Sunday, is the first day of the week. With the coming of Christ the Old Law was abrogated. In the Old Law, God specified that one day was to be kept holy on which He was to be especially worshiped, namely, the Sabbath, our Saturday. But in the New Law, in the Christian Dispensation, Christ gave the power to His Church to determine which day of the week should be kept. The Church by her judicial power decided on Sunday because Christ rose from the dead on Sunday and because the Holy Ghost descended upon the Apostles on Sunday. The Church is our rule of faith, not the Bible. The Bible must be interpreted by the Church, the official infallible teacher of God on earth.

16. *Mr. Blake is a Catholic, but he does not attend Sunday Mass. He says he will work while he is young and strong and will devote a great deal of time to his soul when he is old and can no longer work. What would you tell him?*

How does Mr. Blake know that he will live to be old? Death is very uncertain. Christ tells us that He will come "as the thief in the night"; we know not the day nor the hour. Mr. Blake is like the man in the Gospel who filled his barns and procured all sorts of luxuries for himself, intending to live in ease and comfort for the rest of his days without paying any attention to his soul's welfare during his days of material gain. "Thou fool, this night do they require thy soul of thee" (Luke xii. 20). Mr. Blake is committing the sin of presumption and disobeys the Third Commandment every time he fails in his Sunday obligations.

17. *Marie would not get up at once when her mother called her on Sunday morning. Because of this she came to Mass after the Offertory. What must she do? Why? Suppose there is no other Mass, what obligation has she?*

This question can best be answered in the words of the great theologian, H. Noldin, S.J. (II. 276): "It is not sufficient to assist only at the essential and integral part of the sacrifice, but according to the precept of the Church we must assist at the whole Mass — at the entire liturgical function from the psalm 'Judica' to the priest's blessing inclusive. He who cannot assist at the entire Mass, is bound, if he can, to assist at least at *the essential and integral part* of the Mass, namely, the consecration and Communion; he who cannot assist even at these (two) parts, is not strictly bound to assist at the accidental parts (prayers before the Gospel or prayers after the Communion) since the precept can no longer be fulfilled — at least in substance." To this the theologian Tanquerey (II. 601) adds: "He who was present only at the essential and integral part of the Mass, is bound, if he can, to supply the omitted parts by assisting at another Mass." If these parts were omitted through our own fault, and there is no other Mass, we must confess that we were late for Mass through our own fault.

18. *Mr. Payne goes to Mass and other devotions every Sunday. During the week, however, he is engaged in a dishonest business. What do you think of him as a Christian?*

Mr. Payne is not a practical Catholic. Rather he is like the Pharisees of old. By his dishonest business, he contradicts all that he does in the way of attending Mass, etc., on Sunday. He is like the Pharisees because he honors God only with his lips while his heart is far from Him. He is bound to fulfill the Sunday precept even though he may disregard all the other laws.

19. *What does the Consecration of the Mass mean to you? Why do you look at the Host and whisper, "My Lord and my God"?*

The Consecration means to me that the priest (who takes the place of Christ) changes the bread and wine into the very Body and Blood of Christ, just as Christ Himself did at the Last Supper and commanded likewise His Apostles and successors to do. The Incarnate Christ is brought down upon the altar by the words of consecration pronounced by the priest. I say: "My Lord and my God" to show that I believe that Christ is truly present under the species of bread and wine after the Consecration — it is my act of faith.

8.

THE FOURTH COMMANDMENT OF GOD

Problem Questions, Chap. IX, pp. 76–79.

1. *Did you ever hear a little boy or a little girl call his father by a name that was not nice? Maybe he did not call his father that name so he could hear it, but you heard it. What would you do?*

Tell such a boy or girl that by dishonoring their parents they dishonor God Himself. After our Heavenly Father made us, He gave us a father and mother to take His place and care for us. By obeying and loving our parents, we honor God Himself, and merit His approval. To grieve our parents would be to grieve God. After God we owe most to our parents. Therefore we must reverence and be grateful to them for all that they have done for us. Our parents come next after God — the Fourth Commandment comes immediately after the first three which relate to God. Let us remember, too, that Christ, who was God-Man, obeyed an earthly mother and father. Such language from a child shows great disrespect and ungratefulness to his father. The child should apologize to his father, and also tell what he has done when he goes to confession.

2. *I know a little girl who will not talk to her mother for a long time, even for a whole hour, because mother punished her. What should this girl do to get over her nasty feelings?*

This little girl should tell her mother that she is sorry and that she will not act that way again. She should recall that her parents are the representatives of God Himself. When she dishonors her parents, she dishonors God. She should tell it in confession.

3. *Sometimes a little boy will talk real meanly about his father because his father will not give him a dime to spend for a movie. What do you think of a boy like that? I wonder if you ever did that? Let's tell Jesus today we will never do that again.*

Such a little boy is disrespectful to his father and hence to

God. The father knows what is best for his son. Therefore the boy should obey his father. Let him recall the example of Chris and the saints.

4. *I once saw a little boy run out and slam the door when hi father refused to let him stay on the street with other boys until nine o'clock. What should that boy do to make up for this act?*

That boy should go back and apologize to his father for slamming the door. He should tell it in confession.

5. *When you meet your mother on the street, how should you show your respect to her? I think your mother would almost weep if her little boy would run away when he sees her coming, don't you?*

If you are a boy, tip your hat to your mother and greet her when you meet her on the street. Speak kindly and greet her if you are a girl. Ask her if there is anything you can do to help her.

6. *If mother sometimes does things you know are wrong, for instance, suppose she tells you to stay home from school to help her with the washing and to tell the teacher you were sick, what would you say to mother about it?*

Tell your mother in a kind way that you were taught that such a thing would be a lie, a sin.

7. *If mother dresses in an old-fashioned way, would you be ashamed of her when you are with your friends in a crowd?*

Clothes do not make a person and do not excuse you from respecting your mother's God-given authority. You should not be ashamed of your mother.

8. *Who knows what contempt means? If a child thinks himself so much better and smarter than his parents and acts that way (contempt), he is sinning against the Fourth Commandment through contempt. What does that mean?*

Contempt means disdain, disobedience to lawful orders. If a

child thinks that he is so much smarter and better than his parents, he shows contempt for them. He looks down on them as being ignorant, as being inferior to himself. Hence he does not obey them. Rather he despises his parents, and thereby disobeys and despises God.

9. *What do you think of your big sister who says to mother: "Oh, shucks! you're an old-timer"?*

Your sister is showing contempt for your mother and thereby is disobeying the Fourth Commandment, because she is not showing the proper respect for your mother. She is ashamed of your mother.

10. *Why do you love your mother? Your father?*

I love my mother and father because God has placed them over me to be His representatives. They take His place on earth and hence I must reverence, love, and obey my parents. If I do not obey and love them, I turn away from God by sin. The authority which my parents possess has come from God. Therefore I must respect that authority. Christ loved His Mother, Mary, and His foster father, Joseph. Again, I love my mother because it was she who brought me into this world, who reared and taught me in my early years how to walk, talk, and play. She it was who watched over me when I was sick. She it is who does so many kindnesses for me without my even knowing it. I love my father because he has provided for me both as to body and mind by feeding and clothing me and by giving me a good Christian education.

11. *What do you think of a little girl your age who often says, "Mamma, I love you so much," but always gets pouty when her mother says she should wash the dishes or take care of the baby?*

Such a little girl does not really mean what she says to her mother about loving her. If she did, she would do what her mother asks her to do, willingly and with a smile. Obedience consists not merely in words but in deeds.

12. *When father and mother are old and perhaps poor and you are grown up, what will you do for them?*

I will honor and respect them, support them as far as I am able, and try to make their old age as comfortable as possible.

13. *If mother is very sad because you are not a very good boy or girl, and is worried because you have not been good at school, or have had a fight with the boys, or have taken some money, what do you think you ought to do to make her happy again?*

Go to your mother and tell her from your heart that you are truly sorry for what you have done. Promise her that you will not do it again. Go to confession.

14. *What do you think of your big sister if she tells your mother to go away for the evening because she intends to have "swell" company and is afraid your mother won't be swell enough? Will you ever do that?*

Your big sister is surely guilty of a serious breach of the Fourth Commandment by showing contempt for your mother. No, you will never do that.

15. *George is a little boy who thinks he knows better than his father. His father says to him: "George, I don't want you to go with Billy Jones any more; he's not the kind of boy I want you to be with." But George knows better and won't take his father's advice and goes with Billy Jones. Do you think George loves his father if he won't listen to him?*

George does not love his father, if he will not listen to such good advice, but rather despises him. Neither does he love God because he disobeys His representative.

16. *Mother has made you a dress but you don't like it; how would you show your love and gratitude to her in spite of your feelings?*

Thank her for the dress and wear it cheerfully in spite of your feelings.

17. *Mother is sick and very tired. What will you do when you come home from school to show her that you love her?*

Make a visit to our Lord in the Blessed Sacrament on your way home from school and say a prayer for your mother that she may get well. When you get home, wait on your mother. Do what you can about the house, wash dishes, go to the store, prepare supper, etc.

18. *What are some of the jobs you can do at home to show you love your parents?*

Do errands, wash dishes, mind the baby, empty the ashes, shovel snow, carry coal and wood, cut the grass, rake the yard, ask their advice when in doubt about anything, do what you are told, and treat your parents with the highest respect.

19. *Father says, "You stay home tonight. No movies." Dad and mother go away for the evening and you know it. Joe E. Brown is on just around the corner and you can get back long before your parents come home and they will never know anything about it. Will you go to that movie? What do you think of one who would go after his father has said this?*

No, you will not go to the movie. One who would go in such a case would not only be disobedient to his father, but he would be showing contempt for the God-given authority which his father has. He would be a sneak.

20. *Mother wants you to eat spinach and to drink milk. You don't like it and begin to grumble and get stubborn at the table. You know that is wrong, but you always do it. How can you get over that habit?*

Simply make up your mind that your mother knows what is best for you and that you will not grumble. Eat and drink what your mother wants you to. Think of how good it is, not of how bad it tastes to you. Remember that every kind of food is a gift from God. Ask God to help you overcome your bad habits.

21. *Mother has told her little girl to watch the baby on the lawn. The fire engine comes by and she runs along, forgetting all about the baby. After an hour she comes back. A little voice had whispered to her after a little while that she is disobedient, but she would not listen. Baby is still safe on the lawn. Should the girl tell mother what she had done or should she say nothing about it because the baby's all right? What would you do?*

This girl should tell her mother and tell her that she is sorry for being disobedient.

22. *Sunday afternoon there are services at church. Dad says, "Son, you go to church this afternoon, and then you may go to the park." You run off to church, kneel about two minutes in the back, then run out to the park. Were you obedient?*

No, you were not obedient, because "Dad" certainly intended that you attend the services and not just make a hurried visit to the Church. You have shown disrespect for the services of God's Church.

23. *Father says, "You mow the lawn this morning." You obey but you are grumbling and grouching the whole morning. How are you sinning against the Fourth Commandment?*

In this case you are sinning against the Fourth Commandment by disobedience. "God loves a cheerful giver" — that is, obedience which is given willingly and gladly.

24. *Do you see any rewards God has promised in the Fourth Commandment to children who obey? What are they?*

Yes, a rich reward from God in the next life, and probably a long life, happiness, peace, and safety upon earth.

25. *What punishments has God made ready for those children who are disobedient to their parents in very important cases? Can you tell the class how a big man might commit a mortal sin against his parents?*

Those who do not honor their parents will be punished by God in the next life. They will probably live unhappily and in shame upon earth, and will perhaps come to an unfortunate and miserable end.

A grown man might commit a mortal sin in this respect by refusing to help his parents in their old age, when he is able to and when they are in need, or by showing them great disrespect and dishonor, by quarreling angrily with them.

26. *How long must a boy or girl obey parents?*

Children must obey their parents as long as they are under their authority and control, in all that is not sin.[1]

27. *If a boy of your age usually is disobedient, how can he learn to become obedient?*

By realizing that his parents are God's representatives, by making up his mind to be obedient, by doing what he is told to do without hesitation, unless, of course, it would be a sin. He should follow the example of the child Christ: "He was subject to them."

28. *You don't like your teacher sometimes because you think she is cross. You try to tease her by being naughty and when she calls on you, you get saucy. Why must you obey even a teacher whom you do not like?*

You must obey even a teacher whom you do not like because she is placed in charge of you as your lawful superior. The authority which she has comes ultimately from God. The teacher takes the place of the parent. Hence she must be obeyed.

29. *A girl is stubborn because she thinks she did not deserve to be scolded. Even if she didn't deserve it, what else might she do to show the teacher that she is innocent instead of becoming stubborn?*

She might explain to the teacher that she is innocent and hence did not deserve to be scolded, or she might ask the guilty one to admit his guilt to the teacher.

---

[1] Spirago-Clarke, *The Catechism Explained*, pp. 370, 371.

30. *If you have said something that is very disrespectful about your teacher and which would lower her in the minds of the other children, making them act naughtily, what would you have to do to make up for this?*

If the statement was made in public, you must publicly retract that statement, try to correct what you said, and admit that you were wrong.

31. *You may not take books home from a shelf. You started a story and want to finish it, so you slip the book between your other ones and go off with it, intending to return it in the morning. Is that right?*

This certainly is not obedience. You have disobeyed the rules of your teacher who is your lawful superior.

32. *How do you like this resolution: I am going to obey the rules of the school to keep out of trouble?*

The child should obey the rules of the school because the teacher takes the place of our parents and of God. The trouble that might follow from disobeying these rules is small compared to the punishment that God will inflict upon the disobedient.

33. *Dad has given you five cents to put into the collection box. On the way you buy four cents' worth of candy and put one cent into the box. Besides deceiving, how would you be failing in your duty toward the Church?*

You would also be disobeying the Fifth Commandment of the Church which states that we must contribute to the support of our pastors. You would also be stealing as well as deceiving.

34. *You know you should not talk in church when the Blessed Sacrament is there, but your friend next to you starts talking; what will you do about it?*

Ask him to kindly keep quiet. If he pays no attention to your request and it is possible for you to move, do so. Explain to him later the meaning of the Real Presence in our churches.

35. *Some little boy says very bad things about the priest which he has heard his father say. He is saying this to a crowd of boys and you also hear him. Have you any duty to stop him and how would you do it?*

You have a strict duty in charity to stop that boy, if you think it would do any good to try to stop him. Explain to him the sinfulness of calumny, especially of a priest and of men in influential positions, and the obligation of repairing the injury done to another's good name.

36. *To be a good citizen a boy or girl must always obey the traffic rules; besides running the risk of being hurt, aren't children disobeying at such times if they run their own way as they please? Is that a sin?*

All authority, even that of civil rulers, comes from God. A civil law that is reasonable and made for the good of the people, binds us in conscience. To break it is in some way a sin.

37. *You must help keep the streets clean. After school you have banana peelings, paper bags, etc., which you throw into a back street when nobody sees you. What kind of boy might such continued action make you?*

Such continued action might make you careless later on in observing more serious laws and regulations. Even though no one else sees you throw this refuse in the street, God sees you everywhere. Such actions on your part show that you have a double personality. You do what is right only when you know that you are being watched. You forget that God knows and sees everything you do.

38. *You have chicken pox but you play with the neighbor children anyway when their mother and your mother don't see you. Are you disobeying a law?*

Yes, you are disobeying a law of the health department, which says that you must not mingle with others when you are under quarantine. This law is made for the good of the people. It is reasonable because it aims to protect the lives of others. Hence you are bound in conscience to observe such a law. To break this law is sinful because it was made by legitimate civil rulers who have their authority from God.

9.

THE FIFTH COMMANDMENT OF GOD

Problem Questions, Chap. X, pp. 85, 86.

1. *What do you think is the chief reason we may not kill our neighbors or ourselves?*

The chief reason why we may not kill our neighbors or ourselves is that God is the author of life and death, and to Him alone belongs the right to take away life.

2. *Our body is like a rented house. The owner of the house can do what he wants to with it, but the renter may not. How does a renter treat the house? How, then, should we treat our body?*

The renter must treat the house which he rents in such a way that he will not destroy any part of it. He must take care of it as if it were his own; otherwise he must repair the loss which he causes the owner through his carelessness or neglect. We may apply this to ourselves in regard to the care we should take of our bodies. God gave us the body together with the life that is in it; it belongs to God; we may not use it and dispose of it in any manner whatsoever. He has promised that one day our bodies will be glorified provided we keep His commandments, do His will, and, above all, provided we do not dishonor and desecrate the body by sinful actions.

3. *Many of you have seen a drunken man on the street. What do you think of such a man? Would you like to be a man like that? If not, what must you start doing today already?*

A man who goes so far as to lose control of himself by the use of strong drink is surely not taking care of the body that God gave him, the temple of the Holy Ghost. Surely you do not wish to be like that. Then you must begin now while you are young to mortify yourselves in small things. Give up eating candy once in a while; obey gladly at home when you are asked to do anything. If you begin to mortify yourselves now, you will be able to resist with ease the temptation to strong drink later on in life. Just as consenting to a temptation weakens the will, so the overcoming of a temptation strengthens the will. The will is also strengthened by mortifying and denying ourselves, by giving up from time to time things which are permissible.

4. *Some children think it is "smart" to hang on cars, to run in front of coming automobiles or trains. Are these acts sinful?*

Such children certainly are placing themselves in very great danger of being killed, or badly hurt, and consequently show little respect for the life which God has given them.

5. *A friend has told you that swimming is fine. Your father said the water is still too cold. The boy calls you a coward because you tell him the water is too cold. What will you do about it?*

You should obey your father in such a case, because he surely knows what is best for you. Your father knows that it is dangerous to go swimming in water which is too cold. It may give you a cramp and you might drown as a result of the cramp. Obey your father by all means. You must take care of your health. If you go swimming in this case, you may get a bad cold or even pneumonia. Above all, you are disobeying your father, and by disobeying your father you disobey God Himself.

6. *A friend tells you in the presence of a group of younger children, that one of your classmates has cheated in an examination, has stolen something, has lied. He is not absolutely sure, but he tells it anyway. How can you prevent the sin of scandal with these younger children?*

The friend should not tell these things about his classmate, unless he is sure that they are true. If they are true, he should tell them only when some good would result from his doing so. If he mentions them before younger children, he should at the same time stress the sinful and objectionable features of such actions.

7. *If you told others the same stories about this boy, and they in turn told others, what do you think of the guilt in your case?*

The guilt in your case would be very great. You would be responsible not only for your own sin but in some way for the sins committed by those who repeat the story after you. By acting thus you are destroying the good reputation of another. You are ruining his good name in the eyes of others who perhaps thought well of him. You may also cause him temporal harm. Since you are not sure of what you say in this regard, you may be telling lies. You are giving bad examples to others.

8. *Even if you know these things to be true about him, why should you refrain from telling your friends about them? Whom should you tell?*

Even though you know that these things are true, you should refrain from telling others. If you do tell, you will lessen that person's character in the estimation of others. You will help to destroy his reputation and good name thereby. Instead of telling others what you know, you should go to the person himself and tell him what you have heard. If he admits that it is true, then you should try to convince him that he did wrong and that he should not do it again. Tell him also that he should go to confession.

9. *At times girls are very jealous of one another. When another person receives a reward, how can you overcome your feeling of envy or jealousy? Often say, "Jesus help me to become a noble child."*

Go to the other child who has received the reward and offer him or her your congratulations. This will help you overcome your jealousy. Try to convince yourself that the other child was more deserving than yourself. Ask Jesus to help you become a good and noble child.

10. *I have often heard children say, "I just hate John. I can't stand him." If these children hate the evil qualities of John, does that prove that they hate John himself? In what does the sin consist?*

If these children hate the evil qualities of John, it does not necessarily prove that they hate John himself. We know from experience that we can dislike a person's bad qualities and at the same time like the person himself for his good qualities. The sin consists in hating the person himself, and this is forbidden by the Fifth Commandment of God.

11. *What do you think a good way of treating a child who always picks a quarrel on the playground or in the games?*
Either keep such a child off the playground for a time or try in a polite way to show him that what he does is wrong. Give him the example of Christ and of the saints. Tell him of the other children who play so well together. Make him feel ashamed of himself for acting that way, but do it in a kind way.

12. *Do you think it is a joke to trip anybody purposely? Mention some of the results to such a thoughtless act.*
It is not a very practical joke to trip anybody purposely. Such a thoughtless act may cause serious injury to the person who is tripped. Perhaps it will cripple him for life, or even cause his death.

13. *When you cause suffering through such a foolish joke, are you obliged to pay the bills due to doctors, hospitals, etc.?*
If you foresee that your joke may cause serious injury to the person, you are certainly obliged to pay the doctor, hospital bills, etc., insofar as you are responsible; that is, inasmuch as you helped to bring about the injury. Even if you did not foresee that this might happen, you would probably also be bound to compensate the person for his injury and loss, because such things should have been foreseen as being the probable results of your foolish and thoughtless act.

14. *Sometimes groups of boys or girls talk indecently. You don't want that to continue. How will you try to stop it?*
Tell these boys and girls that they give scandal and bad example to others by their talk. They are defiling their tongues. The tongue is the first member of the body which the priest con-

secrates to God in baptism by placing blessed salt upon it, and should never be used as an instrument of sin. Those who talk indecently cause spiritual damage to others who hear them. Such talk leads others into sin, stains their soul redeemed by the precious Blood of Christ. These boys or girls should remember that in Holy Communion the Body and Blood of Christ is placed upon their tongue and consecrate it to God.

15. *If you have vexed your parents or your schoolmates, what will you do to make up for this?*

Apologize to your parents or your schoolmates for having vexed them, and try not to do this again. Control your temper.

16. *What do you think of a boy who is always calling others names, but who gets very angry as soon as he thinks he is offended?*

He should be instructed to hold his peace and that it is wrong to call others names. Anger is a very dangerous passion and brings about many evil results. Point out to him the example and patience of Christ during His passion and death on the cross. Our Lord was subjected to unbearable agonies and sufferings and yet forgave His enemies who had crucified Him. In the "Our Father" we say: "as we forgive those who trespass against us." If we really mean what we say in this prayer, we will control our temper and not call others names, even though they may offend us. Point out the patience of the saints (St. Stephen being stoned), etc.

17. *What do you think of a boy or a girl who becomes angry very easily?*

A boy or girl who becomes angry very easily is a spoiled child. He or she has probably been allowed to have its own way too much when younger. Point out to him the patience of Christ: the example of St. Francis de Sales.

10.

THE SIXTH AND NINTH COMMANDMENTS

Problem Questions, Chap. XI, pp. 90, 91.

1. *There are three saints always pictured with a lily. Do you know who they are? Why do they carry a lily? Of what is the lily a symbol?*

St. Joseph, St. Aloysius, and St. Anthony. They carry a lily because they preserved their virginity all through their lives. The lily is a symbol of purity.

2. *What is meant by the proverb: Birds of a feather flock together. Do you believe the saying always true? James goes with bad companions, but he says the boys can't harm him; in fact, he is doing his best to make them better. Do you think he will succeed? What comparison could you make to prove your point to James?*

By the proverb "Birds of a feather flock together" is meant that those persons who have the same kind of thoughts and desires, and whose characters are much alike tend to associate with each other. The saying is usually true. Even though James is a good boy himself, he will hardly succeed in making his bad companions good. Rather they will likely make him bad. One bad apple in a box will make all the others bad if it is allowed to remain among the good apples long enough. How much more would this be the case if several apples are bad.

3. *You and your little sister are out in the country for a walk. Your sister is very thirsty and wants to take a drink from the river. Would you allow her to do that? Why not? Would that be worse than to take her to a show that is not good? Or to hear a wicked story, or read a bad book? What difference is there? Do you know of a Scripture text that would apply here?*

You would certainly not allow your little sister to drink from the river because of the great danger of contracting typhoid fever or some other sickness. To allow her to drink from the river would not be any worse than to take your sister to a bad show. In fact it would be worse to take your sister to a bad show. One does harm to the body; the other harms the soul. "Fear ye not them that kill the body, and are not able to kill the soul; but rather fear Him that can destroy both soul and body in hell" (Matt. x. 28).

4. *Ben takes you to his home for the first time and shows you his room. The walls are filled with indecent pictures. Could you judge from them what kind of companion Ben is? Would the pictures be a sure sign that he is bad or could there be another reason for his having them? What should you do in either case?*

You could judge fairly well from the pictures what kind of companion Ben is. Pictures are intended to inspire and aid thought. These pictures show on what his mind feeds. They would be almost a sure sign that he is not the right kind of companion to go with, and that there is something wrong with him morally. Either he is badly instructed or he is bad outright. There could hardly be any other reason for his having such pictures. Give Ben up as a companion because he may be the cause of your spiritual ruin as well as the cause of your physical ruin.

5. *Ann and her sister go to a party. They soon learn that the people at the party are not behaving decently. Ann wants to go home, but her sister says they would offend their friends by leaving now, and furthermore they would be laughed at. What would you do under the circumstances?*

I would leave the party, if it were at all possible without offending the host and hostess. There is danger of false human respect here. If I saw that I could not stay without danger of sin, I would leave, no matter what others would say. People who allow indecent things to happen at parties which they give should not be among those whom I call my friends.

6. *Jack was sitting by the window and reading. All of a sudden he caught himself in the act of daydreaming and realized that his thoughts had drifted to forbidden things. Had Jack committed a sin up to this time? What should he do now? He takes up his book and begins to read again, but finds that he cannot get rid of his evil thoughts. Can you suggest other remedies?*

No, Jack had not committed sin up to the time that he realized what he was doing. He should put the thoughts of such things out of his mind. He should resume his reading if it is a good book that he has. If what he is reading is the cause of his bad thoughts, he should get rid of the book and do something else. He should recall the omnipresence of God and pray to the Blessed Virgin and to his guardian angel to help him get rid of such thoughts. He should take up some other kind of occupation so as to center his mind on something else.

7. *Frank is a lazy boy who spends most of his time in idle dreaming or lying around doing nothing. Joseph, his brother, is always occupied with something. He is always reading, or working, or playing. Which of the two boys has the better chance of remaining morally good? Why? Can you find a proverb that will answer this question?*

Joseph has a better chance of remaining morally good; there is not so much chance for him to be tempted on matters of the Sixth Commandment as long as he keeps his mind busily occupied with other things. Frank will more easily succumb to temptation when it comes because he does nothing to occupy himself, and the devil has an easier task of tempting him and inducing him to sin. The proverb is: "An idle mind is the devil's workshop."

8. *Dorothy is not careful about dressing modestly. Her mother tells her she is doing wrong, but Dorothy answers that she is only doing what other girls are doing and that it has not harmed her yet, nor will it harm her. Do you agree? Do you know that the "Sunday Visitor" is carrying on a crusade for modesty in dress? Look it up and see whether you would like to join.*

Dorothy may be giving scandal. She is presuming too much on

her own strength in overcoming temptation; God gives His grace to the humble.

9. *Grace's older sister wants her to go along to a dance. Grace knows that the place has a very bad reputation, but her sister says that they will stay with their own group and that, after all, it's up to a girl to keep her place. Do you think Grace should go?*

Grace should not go to the dance, neither should her sister. There is always the danger that such a place will be an occasion of sin; and we are bound to avoid occasions of sin.

10. *If your parents or your pastor warned you that the water you were about to drink is poisoned, would you drink the water anyway, just because you could see nothing wrong with it? Do you think people who want to poison others through bad reading would be foolish enough to label the books "Poison"? Do they want you to see that they are bad? Then do you think it wise not to listen to the warning of your parents or your pastor in regard to dangerous amusements, such as dances, movies, etc.?*

If you were told that the water you were about to drink is poisoned, you would not drink it. You would believe your parents. Perhaps you would have the water chemically analyzed to determine whether it contains poison. People who want to poison others through bad reading do not label the books "Poison." If they did, others would not read the books. Such people tell others that the books are worth while and that they contain information which all should know, etc. It is wise to listen to the warnings of your parents and pastor in regard to bad books, dangerous amusements (dances, movies, etc.). They are older than you, and have seen what evil consequences often result from a disregard of the occasion of sin.

11. *Why did God choose Mary as His Mother and St. Joseph as His foster father? Why was He particularly fond of St. John and of little children? Do you know what special favor virgins will enjoy in heaven? Who were the Vestal Virgins, and what favors did they enjoy?*

Christ chose Mary as His Mother and St. Joseph as His foster father because they were both pure and holy and were virgins. Christ was particularly fond of St. John and of little children because they were pure of heart. Heaven is for those who are like children in regard to their simplicity and purity of heart. The state of virginity is much higher than the married state as is attested from Scripture and the Fathers. The Council of Trent (C. 24, 10) states: "It is better and more blessed to remain in virginity or in celibacy than to be united in matrimony." The virgins will enjoy a higher place in heaven even perhaps than the angels because they have had to combat their evil tendencies while the angels do not have concupiscence to contend with. The virgins alone will sing the special canticle before the throne of God (of which St. John speaks in the Apocalypse, xiv, 1–5).

In Roman antiquity the Vestal Virgins were the priestesses of Vesta (the goddess of the hearth and the hearth-fire), set apart to watch the shrines, keep up the sacred fire on the altar, perform the sacrifices, offer up the special prayers for the state, and take part in the festivals of the goddess. A vestal who broke her vow of chastity was buried alive.

12. *Do you know of any great sinners who have become saints? The act of consecration to the Blessed Virgin has been highly recommended by priests to those who wish to free themselves from sins against the Sixth Commandment or to protect themselves against such sins. Say it every day with all your heart, especially when you find yourself in danger.*

Mary Magdalen, St. Augustine.

11.

THE SEVENTH AND TENTH COMMANDMENTS

Problem Questions, Chap. XII, pp. 95–97.

1. *Mother has given you a dollar to buy groceries. The sale today saves you ten cents. What will a truly honest boy do? What do you say about the boy who would spend it for candy without his mother's knowledge?*

A truly honest boy will bring his mother the change and tell her of the saving because of the sale. The boy who would spend the ten cents for candy without his mother's knowledge would be dishonest and would do wrong. He should remember that for every small theft he will have to suffer in purgatory. Little by little he may take more and finally become a thief.

2. *What would you say about putting that money into the mite box in school without your mother's knowledge?*

To put the money in the mite box at school without your mother's knowledge would not be the right thing to do. You should first get your mother's permission to do so. Otherwise it is stolen money that you are giving. Such an act never brings anyone any merit.

3. *Even though stealing a pencil or some paper from a friend is not a serious sin, still you know that it is wrong. Why should you not take it?*

You should not take it because "it offends God venially." Such an act will lead to greater dishonesty later on in life. Besides, for every venial sin you commit you will have to suffer in purgatory.

4. *What may happen to a child who has the habit of taking little things from his neighbor in school without asking his permission?*

Such a child may grow up to be a thief and may come to a

bad end. Big things usually have small beginnings. Honesty is a virtue which everyone should strive to attain and keep. This child should remember that God is present everywhere and knows all things. Even though his neighbor in school does not miss the little things he takes, God will hold the child accountable for such acts at the Judgment.

5. *If you know that a certain girl is taking things from the other pupils, will you keep still about it as long as your things are not taken? Whom should you tell?*

You should not keep still about the matter as long as your things are not taken; but you should first tell that certain girl to own up to what she has done and make good for what she has taken. If she will not do so, probably you should tell those who have had things taken by her, or tell the teacher. Try to make that girl realize that she is cultivating a very bad habit which may ultimately bring her to disgrace. Above all, she offends the all-seeing God every time she takes what does not belong to her, and will not be pardoned by Him until she gives back the stolen things.

6. *Tell the children what you would say to a pupil in your class who took your pencils a number of times and has not returned them.*

You should not keep these things because they do not belong to you. You are retaining without my permission something that belongs to me and you must return it. The Seventh Commandment demands that you return what you have taken, and God will not forgive you until you have done so.

7. *You know your little friend has taken a quarter from his home and bought some candy. He offers to treat you. Are you stealing by taking some of it? How would you make him realize that this is very wrong?*

Yes, you are stealing if you take some of the candy. To make him realize that what he did was wrong, you must refuse to eat any of his candy and tell him that you do so because it is stolen goods. Although he may fool his parents who will not find out that he stole from them, he cannot fool God who knows all things.

8. *You read or hear so often about robberies, especially in the large cities. What is robbery and what kind of sin is it?*

Robbery is the unjust taking of another's goods openly and with violence and without the owner's permission and in his presence. Robbery is frequently a mortal sin.

9. *What is the difference between robbery and theft?*

For the definition of robbery see answer in No. 8 above. Theft is the unjust taking of another's property secretly, while the owner is absent, or at least without the owner's permission.

10. *This last Christmas robbers broke into an orphanage and stole the orphans' gifts and goodies, even some of their clothes. Did they commit a graver sin than if they had stolen from other children?*

Yes, the robbers in this case did commit a graver sin than if they had taken the things from other children, because what the orphans had obtained was given them in charity, could not easily be replaced, and yet was very necessary for them, as the clothes.

11. *What kind of sin is it to steal from the Church, something that belongs to the Church? Is it always a mortal sin?*

To steal from the Church is a sacrilege, but it is not always a mortal sin.

12. *Very often when people go traveling, they will take towels, napkins, spoons, and suchlike, as souvenirs from places they visit. Is this stealing?*

Yes, this is stealing, because they are taking things that do not belong to them. They will be held accountable by God for their actions.

13. *Just a few years ago many babies died in New York. It was proved that the milk which the mothers bought for them was not pure and nutritious enough. It had been adulterated and so the mothers were cheated. Who is guilty before God for so many deaths?*

Those who sold the milk to the mothers are guilty before God for the deaths of those babies. They will have to account for their cheating when they stand before Christ for judgment. Their ill-gotten money will do them no good then.

14. *A merchant has been using incorrect weights for defrauding the people. What can you say about such methods?*

Such methods are dishonest. He cannot fool God who knows all things. The merchant who uses such methods must make good in some way for the weight he has cheated the customers of. He not only commits sin, but he can be punished by the law of the state and city in which he lives.

15. *You have a counterfeit dollar and know it. You got it from somebody else in change. You will be the loser if you do not use it to pay your debt. What will you do in the case?*

It is better not to pay your debt with the counterfeit dollar because if you use it to pay your debt with, the debt will not be paid, and you will still be bound in justice to pay the debt. It is better to tell the person to whom you owe the debt about the matter and promise to pay him as soon as you are able. If you use the counterfeit money to pay the debt, you are cheating and hence you commit a sin.

16. *The conductor has forgotten to collect your fare. Should you pay him of your own accord?*

Yes, pay your fare of your own accord: otherwise you are not honest.

17. *Many men make money by gambling. They are Catholics and go to Church regularly. What might Protestants say on this point about the Catholic Church? What do you say?*

The Protestants might object: "There is the Catholic Church

for you, the Catholics go to church and hear one thing and then practice another." We reply that it is not the fault of the Church if some of her members do things which are wrong. She tells her members what they should and must do to get to heaven and gives them the means (sacraments) to do so. If they fail, it is the fault of the individual and not of the Church. The Church remains divine.

18. *Mr. Frank is always grumbling about paying his school taxes and assessments, saying he has no children in school. Why do you think he is doing wrong?*

Mr. Frank is doing wrong because he is bound to support the schools of his community as long as he is able to do so, even though he has no children of his own attending them. Schools are for the common welfare of the community. He will be held accountable by God for the use he has made of his money. "What doth it profit a man, if he gain the whole world, and suffer the loss of his own soul?" (Matt. xvi. 26.)

19. *In a very famous letter to the world, called an encyclical, Pope Leo XIII, our Holy Father, said, "Every wage earner is entitled to a just wage." What do you think he meant? Explain also how the wage earner must be just to his employer.*

When the Holy Father said that every wage earner is entitled to a just wage, he meant that the employer is bound in justice to pay his employees enough so that they can support their families in ordinary comfort and have a few things more than the mere necessities of life. He must pay him for the work that he does according to the common standards of justice.

The wage earner must be just to his employer; that is, he is bound in justice to do his work well and not to waste time for which he is being justly paid by the employer. He is bound in conscience to give his services to his employer during the times in which he is employed and to do his work as well as he can.

20. *Whenever you have found something of great or small value, what should you do?*

You should try to find the owner of the article you have found.

If he shows up, you must in justice give the article back to him, when he pays you for whatever expense you may have had in trying to locate him, such as putting an ad in the newspaper, etc. One is not entitled in justice to a reward, however, unless the owner promises one. If the owner cannot be found after diligent search, you may keep the article.

21. *You and another boy have been trying to win the highest honors in your class. Both of you have worked very, very hard. He wins. A temptation to wish him all kinds of bad things comes upon you, but you heroically overcome it and are kind and good to him. Who is the greater hero in God's eyes?*

You are the greater hero in the eyes of God because you have done a noble deed. It takes a great deal of humility to do such a thing. You will receive a greater reward in heaven.

22. *How do you think a child will grow up who is never satisfied with what he has but always wants more and more?*

Such a child will grow up to be avaricious, jealous, envious, and miserly. He will never be satisfied in later life with what he has; but he will desire to have the property of others as his own.

23. *When you are tempted to desire something unlawfully, how about thinking like this: "No person knows my thoughts, but there is One who examines my mind and heart — God"?*

Such a thought is a wholesome one and brings with it God's grace. If you keep this thought in mind and realize what it means, you need have no fear for the future. God will reward you a hundredfold.

24. *Does the Tenth Commandment forbid one to desire great advancement in one's work or in acquiring property?*

To desire to advance in one's work, if it be legitimate advancement and for the glory of God, is not forbidden by the Tenth Commandment; but to want to advance at the expense and to the detriment of someone else is wrong. To desire to acquire property is legitimate as long as it does not interfere with our spiritual life and does no harm to anyone else; but such a desire may lead one into sins of injustice and hence is to be avoided. It is not in keeping with the Beatitude, "Blessed are the poor in spirit."

25. John has cut a little hole in his school desk. Day by day it gets a little larger. Is he committing sin?

Yes, he is probably committing sin, at least venial, if he realizes that what he does is wrong. He is willfully destroying property that does not belong to him. He will have to suffer in purgatory for his sin.

26. You see a boy marking up some of the schoolbooks with ink. What are you going to do about that, or isn't it any of your business?

It is your business to tell that child that he is doing wrong and that he is destroying property that does not belong to him. It belongs to you just as much as it belongs to him because the schoolbooks in such a case belong to the taxpayers.

27. On your way home from school every evening a group of boys do something wrong and think it is a good joke; for instance, they mark up or smear walls of buildings, steal fruit from a stand or from an orchard, tear each other's clothing, break down fences. You know all these things are wrong. What could you do about it?

Remind the group of boys that they are willfully destroying property that does not belong to them and that they are bound in justice to make good for the damage they do. They are stealing.

28. At times a child is found in school who is happy when he can damage property. He lets the faucet open, writes on the walls, breaks locks, etc. How could you other boys help him to stop this?

First remind him that God sees him at whatever he does. God will not forgive him unless he makes restitution for the damage he has caused. Try to show him that such actions are wrong and that he is misusing things that do not belong to him.

29. *You have borrowed a book from your friend. Of course, you mean to restore it, but months have slipped by and the book is showing pretty hard use. How are you failing in showing respect to your neighbor's property?*

You are failing to show respect for your neighbor's property because when you use something that belongs to another, you are bound to take good care of it and see to it that it is returned in as good condition as it was when you received it. You must make up for the damage you do. God will not forgive you until you repair the damage you have caused.

12.

THE EIGHTH COMMANDMENT

Problem Questions, Chap. XIII, pp. 102, 103.

1. *A friend of yours is passing notes to others and does not pass them to you. You feel sure that she is telling things about you. Are you justified in drawing such conclusions? What sin do you commit? Can you give other examples of rash judgment.*

Certainly not. The sin of rash judgment. Other examples:

a) A classmate receives unusually good marks in one class for a month. You feel sure that he must have cheated.

b) A boy or girl whom you saw going to confession on the previous evening stays away from Holy Communion in the morning. You conclude he must have fallen into grave sin since yesterday.

2. *A boy in your class has been found guilty of stealing. A few days later you miss some money out of your desk. You and your classmates conclude that the same boy stole your money. What should you do about it? Discuss fully.*

Your conclusion is too hasty. It is quite possible that the boy steals no more since he has been found out. Again, your money may have been taken by another who expected the suspicion to fall on the former thief; or it may have been mislaid, by yourself or by another, quite accidentally. Since you had no proof that the boy actually took it, you and your classmates judged rashly, and you should tell them so.

3. *Your mother sends you to the door to tell an agent that she is not at home. Should you obey?*

   a) Must children obey their parents in all things? Can you give an example of a case in which a child need not obey its parents?

   b) Do you think there is any difference between lies that are harmless and those that are not? What would you consider a harmless lie? A harmful lie?

Yes, because your mother undoubtedly means that she is not there to be troubled by agents. In other words, the common phrase "not at home" in this case means "not to be bothered." Most of the agents understand it that way, and hence are not being deceived at all.

   a) Children are bound to obey their parents in all things except sin. You need not obey, for example, if they command you to stay away from Mass on Sunday when there is nothing else to prevent you from hearing Mass that day.

   b) There is a difference between lies that are harmful and those that are not. A harmless lie is a simple untruth which is not said seriously or not taken seriously, for example, the story that Santa Claus brings presents at Christmas time; or some story that never happened, told in the first person for the sake of humor. A harmful lie is one that is told seriously for the purpose of deceiving another or injuring another.

4. *The teacher leaves the classroom and asks all the children to keep on working quietly. As soon as she is out you turn around and laugh and talk. When she returns you quickly get back to your work. Is there any wrong in that? What should you call such action?*

Yes, there is. Such action is called hypocrisy, or pretense to goodness which you have not. Although you may fool the teacher, you cannot fool God who is everywhere present and who knows all things.

5. Mary knows that Ethel is in bad company and is deceiving her teacher and her parents. Should she tell anyone? Should we always tell when we know something about another person?

If the matter is serious, she should first of all consult her confessor about it. Most likely he would advise her to tell the teacher or the girl's parents, provided (*a*) she knows that it would do some good to tell them, and provided (*b*) she could do so without much difficulty or harm to herself. Indeed not, for it is very seldom that any good can be achieved thereby. Telling it merely for the sake of spreading the information you have, would be a sin of detraction.

6. You have a chance to look into your book during examination. May you do so?

Certainly not. Dishonesty like that is never allowed.

7. The girl sitting behind you in school does not know her lesson. You can help her out by opening your book and placing it so that she can see the lesson. May you help her? Who do you think would be wronged more by such an action, the teacher or the girl?

No. The girl would be wronged the more by such an action, since it would lead her to dishonesty and possibly to the loss of a proper education. Such an action would wrong the teacher also because it would prevent her from getting a correct estimate of the girl's knowledge and application, something that she has a right to know.

8. One of the boys in your school is arrested for forgery. Everybody knows about it. May you discuss the matter?

You may not discuss the matter merely to take pleasure in the other boy's misfortune. Since everybody knows about it, however, there is nothing wrong in discussing it charitably.

9. *You play sick so that you don't have to go to school. Is there any wrong in that?*

Yes, there is. It is an act of dishonesty and therefore a sin. Dishonest action like that is just as bad as dishonest words, or lying. Remember, that you cannot fool God.

10. *Elsie has a new dress. She asks you how you like it. You do not like it at all, but you do not wish to hurt her feelings. How would you answer her?*

Forget for the moment the things you do not like about the dress and express your appreciation of those that you do like. Certainly there must be something on the dress to please anyone: if it is not the color, it may be the cut; if it is not the cut, it may be the trimming or the texture of the material or, perhaps, the buttons. Such a practice will also tend to sharpen your sense of observation.

11. *Your friend Margaret tells you a secret and asks you never to tell. You promise. Must you keep your word?*

Generally speaking, people should never pry into the secrets of others and very seldom receive them under promise not to tell, because secrets once known are extremely hard to keep to ourselves. However, since you have already learned her secret and promised never to tell, you are bound under pain of sin to keep the promise, unless, of course, the secret is about something that would cause serious harm to you or to others if it were not revealed. The secrets of children, however, are frequently unimportant, and hence the promise to keep such secrets does not bind very seriously.

12. *Your chum received a letter which she does not show you. You go to her desk later and read the letter without her consent or knowledge. Had you a right to do so?*

Indeed not. To read personal letters of others who are in no way committed to your care, without their knowledge, is just as unjust as stealing their property, because the contents of their letters is their own until they give it out themselves.

13. *A boy asks you where you are going. You tell him you are going to the North Pole. Is that a lie?*

It is not a lie because the boy knows well enough that you are only jesting, and hence is not deceived at all.

14. *You listen with pleasure to an evil story about someone else. Do you commit any wrong?*

You commit a wrong against charity, since you approve of the evil story. Moreover, you co-operate in the other person's sin of detraction.

13.

SIN

Problem Questions, Chap. XIV, p. 114.

1. *What is the relation of sin to the commandments?*

The commandments are the signposts along the highway that leads to God. They are set there by God Himself to direct the wayfaring soul of man along the one and only road to his proper end and eternal happiness. They point out the way for those who seek it and guide those who are on it lest they wander astray and get lost. Man is free to follow these signposts or to disregard them according to his own choosing. If he follows them faithfully, he is assured of reaching the destination; if he disregards them and goes astray he does so to his own woe, for by his own guilt he forfeits the only means of attaining his eternal happiness. This guilt of going astray by violating God's commandments is the guilt of sin.

2. *What is sin?*

Sin is the willful transgression, or violation, of God's law.

3. *What are the occasions of sin?*

The occasions of sin are those persons, places, things, situations, and circumstances which have led one into sin in the past or are likely to lead one into sin in the future.

4. *In what ways may a person co-operate in the sins of another?*

A person may co-operate in the sins of another by advice, by command, by consent, by provocation, by praise or flattery, by silence, by connivance, by taking any part in the sin itself, or by defending the sinful action.

5. *Give a concrete example.*

A concrete example — a sin against the Tenth Commandment:

a) Two boys go out on Halloween and come to a large street lamp. John, the younger by four years, says to the other, "Bob, let's have some fun and smash up this lamp." (He is sinning by advice.)

b) Bob knows that it is a sin to destroy another's property, and should say so to the younger boy; but he keeps quiet. (He is sinning by silence.)

c) John thinks about it himself and asks, "Do you think it would be wrong?" And Bob, who knows well enough, answers, "I don't know." (He sins by connivance.)

d) Then he looks up at the lamp and says, "It might not be exactly all right; but this is Halloween, so we can forget the Catechism for once." (He is defending the sin.)

e) The younger lad protests: "I ain't going to do it if it's wrong." Whereupon Bob grins at him and teases, "Ah, you're scared to do it, that's all." (He sins by provocation.)

f) John tries to excuse himself: "I can't throw straight enough to hit it, anyway." "Yes, you can," says the elder. "I saw you pitching ball last summer and you had it all over the other kids. Dad says you'll be in the Leagues some day." (He is sinning by praise and flattery.)

g) John likes that and begins to feel like somebody, so he gets louder: "I don't care, but I'm not going to throw at that lamp." Then Bob catches him by the collar and shakes him. "You'll have to," he orders, "or I'll rub your face in the fresh tar on the next street corner!" (He is sinning by command.)

h) John, however, frees himself and runs away. At the corner he meets Jim, who lives close by, and both of them watch Bob throw pebbles at the lamp. John says to Jimmy, "Look at him wasting his time with those bits of gravel! If he were smarter he'd get a brick." (Advice again.) "Say, we've got some bricks in our back yard," Jim suggests. "Shall I get some for him?" (He intends to take part in the sin.)

i) John thinks that would be an easy way to make up with Bob, so he agrees: "Sure, get a couple. I'll go with you." (And

he sins by consent.) Bob smashes the lamp, but John and Jim
are also guilty by co-operating in the sin.

6. *Show in a particular case how the person who co-operates in a
sin may be the real sinner.*

From the foregoing example we can easily see how each boy
was a real sinner. If Bob, who was the oldest, would have minded
his Catechism, he should have let the lamp alone and persuaded
the others to do likewise. But he committed a real sin in destroying the lamp for the sake of foolish fun. John and Jim were also
real sinners because they consented to the sin and assisted Bob
in the act.

7. *What was Adam's sin in the Garden of Eden?*

Adam's sin in the Garden of Eden was a willful sin of pride and
disobedience.

8. *Is it in its nature the same kind of sin we commit when we
sin?*

In its nature Adam's sin was the same kind of sin we commit
when we sin; that is, a personal sin. Original sin, however, as it
is transmitted to us with our human nature, is not personal but
inherited.

9. *What is actual sin? Was Adam's sin an actual sin?*

Actual sin is a personal willful violation of God's law. Adam's
sin was an actual sin.

10. *What is original sin? What are its effects on us?*

Original sin is the guilty state of soul which we inherit with
nature from Adam, the head of the whole human race, because
of his transgression. The effects of original sin upon us are:

a) The loss of sanctifying grace, and the habitual aversion
from God which follows upon that loss.

b) The loss of the preternatural gifts that our first parents
enjoyed before the fall, and the consequent subjection to concupiscence, death, and all the other pains and miseries of life.

11. *What is the difference between mortal and venial sin?*

"Mortal sin is a conscious and deliberate violation of God's law by one who is aware of the *grave* obligation involved." "Venial sin is a conscious and deliberate violation of God's law by one who is aware of the *lesser* obligation involved."[1]

12. *What three conditions of an act make it a mortal sin?*

The three conditions of an act that make it a mortal sin are: (*a*) grievous matter; (*b*) sufficient reflection; (*c*) full consent of the will.

13. *What are the seven capital sins? Are they sins in the same sense as we have been using the term?*

The seven capital sins are: (1) Pride, (2) Covetousness, (3) Lust, (4) Anger, (5) Gluttony, (6) Envy, (7) Sloth. These are not sins in the same sense as we have been using the term; they are, rather, sources and fountains of the other sins and vices.

14. *Show how any (each) one of the capital sins leads to actual sins.*

(1) A proud person desires his own excellence to such an extent that he neglects the proper worship of God, disobeys his parents and superiors, grows ambitious, vainglorious, and boastful about himself.

(2) A covetous person disorderly desires temporal good things and thus becomes stingy and hard-hearted toward the poor, and often resorts to cheating, theft, and many other injustices in order to enrich himself.

(3) A lustful person has a disorderly desire for pleasures of the flesh and so falls into all kinds of impurities; his mind becomes blind to spiritual things; he loses the fear of God, neglects his religion, and often dies in impenitence.

(4) An angry person has a disorderly desire for revenge and thus engages in quarrels, falls into cursing and blaspheming, harbors strong hatred for those he dislikes, and sometimes becomes so violent as to commit murder.

---

[1]Gasparri: *The Catholic Catechism*, Part Two, Chap. IX; Part Three, Chap. XI.

(5) A gluttonous person has an unreasonable desire for food and drink and so falls into overeating, drunkenness, and idleness; his mind becomes dull and he lapses into all kinds of foolish and often obscene talk.

(6) An envious person is depressed or sad because others possess spiritual or temporal things that make him appear less excellent, and so he falls into hatred, detraction, and calumny, finds pleasure in his neighbor's misfortune and feels distressed at his prosperity.

(7) A slothful person is sad about spiritual and temporal good things because they involve labor, and so he neglects his spiritual duties and becomes indifferent toward religion; he falls into cheating and often ruins the property of others.

15. *What do you mean by virtue?*

Virtue is a habit that leads a person to do good and avoid evil.

16. *What are the four cardinal virtues? Illustrate from your experience or reading.*

The four cardinal virtues are: (*a*) Prudence, (*b*) Justice, (*c*) Temperance, (*d*) Fortitude.

a) *Prudence:* Tommy used to attend a certain theater regularly because he usually found an exciting "movie" in it. After a while, however, he noticed that almost after every show he was beset by all kinds of impure thoughts and desires. Being a clever boy, Tommy concluded that that theater was a sure occasion of sin for him, and so decided to attend it no more. In this he certainly exercised the virtue of prudence.

b) *Justice:* Lucille went to a grocery store to get something for her mother. She bought the thing, paid for it, and got back some change. On the way home she counted the money and found that the clerk had given her a dollar more than was coming to her. She hurried back to the store and returned the extra dollar. By this act she practiced justice.

c) *Temperance:* When Anne was fourteen years of age her mother and her elder sister prepared a birthday banquet for her and her friends. When the party began Anne saw a table full of the choicest things that she always liked, and she thought what a joy it would for her to partake of them until she could possibly eat no more! But Anne was temperate and ate no more than ordinarily.

d) Fortitude: Tommy wanted to study medicine and become a doctor. His parents were glad to see him inclined that way, but they were poor and could not pay for his studying at the local college. There was a distant college, however, which was considerably cheaper and in which Tommy could partly work his way through school. But for Tommy that meant leaving the "old gang," denying himself certain pleasures he had at home, and a good amount of extra work. Still he thought of his duty to God, to his parents, and to himself, and went to that distant school. He practiced fortitude.

17. Show how a real love of God in your heart will keep you from sin.

When we really love someone we are ever watchful not to displease him or to offend him in any way. We are eager to carry out whatever that person may wish. Hence when we really love God as we would a most excellent friend and a most loving and generous Father, we also do all that we can to please Him, and try never to do anything that might offend Him. Thus our love for God keeps us from falling into sin.

18. If you are deliberating on an act is it better to say "I won't do this because it is a sin," or "I will do the opposite because of love of God"?

It is better to say, "I will do the opposite because of love of God."

19. Give from literature any character that illustrates the seven capital sins. How does the author make the character unlovely (repulsive)?

PRIDE: Lady Macbeth: Shakespeare's *Macbeth* (cf. Act I, sc. 5 and 7; Act II, sc. 1; Act III, sc. 4; and Act V, sc. 1).

AVARICE: Shylock: Shakespeare's *Merchant of Venice* (cf. Act I, sc. 3; Act III, sc. 1; and Act IV, sc. 1).

LUST: Cleopatra: Shakespeare's *Anthony and Cleopatra* (cf. Act I, sc. 1, 3, and 5; Act II, sc. 5; Act III, sc. 3, 6, 11, 12, and 15; and Act IV, sc. 2).

ENVY: Iago: Shakespeare's *Othello* (cf. Act I, sc. 1; Act II, sc. 1; Act III, sc. 3; Act IV, sc. 1 and 2; and Act V, sc. 1).

GLUTTONY: Nero: Henryk Sienkiewicz's *Quo Vadis?* (cf. Part I, Chap. VII; Part II, Chaps. VIII, IX, XIV; Part III, Chaps. IV, XIII, XV, XIX, XXIX, and Epilogue).

ANGER: Heathcliff: Emily Bronte's *Wuthering Heights* (cf. Chaps. VII, VIII, IX, XI, XIV, XV, XVIII, XXVII, XXVIII, XXIX, and XXXIII).

SLOTH: Petronius: Henryk Sienkiewicz's *Quo Vadis?* (cf. Part I, Chaps. I and III; Part II, Chaps. VII, VIII, X, XIII and XVII; Part III, Chaps. VI, VIII, XXX, XXXI).

14.

THE MESSIAH

Problem Questions, Chap. XV, p. 119.

1. *Make a list of the Old Testament prophecies that you know by heart, regarding the Messiah.*

"I will put enmities between thee and the woman, and thy seed and her seed" (Gen. iii. 15).

"And in thy seed shall all the nations of the earth be blessed, because thou hast obeyed My voice" (Gen. xxii. 18).

"And thou, Bethlehem Ephrata, art a little one among the thousands of Juda: out of thee shall He come forth unto me that is to be the ruler in Israel: and His going forth is from the beginning, from the days of eternity" (Mich. v. 2).

"Behold a virgin shall conceive, and bear a son, and His name shall be called Emmanuel" (Isa. vii. 14).

"The Lord hath said to Me: Thou art My son, this day have I begotten Thee" (Ps. ii. 7).

"For a Child is born to us, and a Son is given to us, and the government is upon His shoulder: and His name shall be called Wonderful, Counselor, God the Mighty, the Father of the world to come, the Prince of Peace" (Isa. ix. 6).

"The Lord hath sworn, and He will not repent: Thou art a priest forever according to the order of Melchisedech" (Ps. cix. 4).

"They parted My garments amongst them, and upon My vesture they cast lots" (Ps. xxi. 19).

"But He was wounded for our iniquities, He was bruised for our sins: the chastisement of our peace was upon Him, and by His bruises we are healed" (Isa. liii. 5).

"And the Lord was pleased to bruise Him in infirmity: if He shall lay down His life for sin, He shall see a long-lived seed, and the will of the Lord shall be prosperous in His hand" (Isa. liii. 10).[1]

2. *What does the word Messiah mean?*

The word Messiah, or Messias, means "The Anointed One," from the Hebrew "maschach," to anoint.

3. *What did the Jews of Christ's day think the kingdom of God would be?*

The Jews of Christ's time thought the kingdom of God would be a restored kingdom of Israel here on earth — a political kingdom which would excel all the other kingdoms and empires of the world in size, in power, in wealth, and in universal prosperity.

4. *Did the people of Christ's day recognize Him as the Messiah?*

Many people of Christ's day recognized Him as the Messiah (John i. 41, 45, 49).

5. *Why was the coming of the Messiah a greater event even than the gift to Moses of the Ten Commandments?*

The Ten Commandments which Moses received were only a

---

[1]Cf. R. G. Bandas, *Biblical Questions*, Vol. I, Chapter "Christ in Prophecy."

few cold laws, or guides, intended to direct men along the way of salvation, but offering no living example of how God wants us to live that law, nor possessing any power in themselves of reconciling the human race with God by removing original sin. In Christ, on the other hand, not only did we receive into our midst the Author of all law and all truth, who revealed to us the whole law in a language that all could understand, but in Him also we have a perfect example of how we should live in order that we may please God and be saved. And above all, He undertook the task of expiating the sins of the whole race and of reconciling us with God by the supreme sacrifice of Himself on the cross; and having thus opened heaven for us and won an infinite treasure of merit for all men, He founded and left us His Church, where He continues to abide with us and in us to the end of time and where He continues to apply His merits to every believing soul through the sacraments. Thus we see that Christ's coming was a far greater event than the gift to Moses of the Ten Commandments.

15.

PREPARE YE THE WAY OF THE LORD

Problem Questions, Chap. XVI, pp. 126, 127

1. *What extraordinary, in fact, supernatural events attended the birth of Christ?*

On the night of Christ's birth an angel, surrounded by the brightness of God, appeared to the shepherds who were watching their flocks near Bethlehem, and announced to them that the Savior, who is Christ the Lord, was born that night and also told where they should go to find Him. Then a multitude of other angels joined him and sang: "Glory be to God in the highest, and on earth peace to men of good will." These events were truly extraordinary and supernatural.

Then, too, the star which appeared to the Wise Men and directed them to the Christ Child, although it may have been but one of the many natural stars as some writers believe, was nevertheless extraordinary in that it led the Wise Men from a great distance precisely to the place where our Lord was at the time. It is believed to have appeared at the very time of Christ's birth.[1]

2. *What does "annunciation" mean? How many annunciations were there in fact? Why do we call the announcement to Mary, the Annunciation?*

"Annunciation" means the act of announcing or proclaiming something. There were actually three annunciations made by angels to men about the time of Christ's birth: (*a*) the one about the birth of John the Baptist made to Zachary; (*b*) the one made to the Blessed Virgin Mary that she was chosen to be the mother of Jesus; and (*c*) the one about the birth of the Savior made to the shepherds.

The announcement made to our Lady is called "The Annunciation" because of its superior dignity and importance. At this Annunciation Mary consented to become the mother of God, and at the very moment of her consent the Incarnation took place by the power of the Holy Ghost.

3. *Compare the reception of the announcement to Mary and to Zachary.*

At both annunciations we find that the appearance of the angel startles his hearers. Zachary is troubled because of the very appearance of the angel, while Mary in her humility is startled rather at the highly laudatory words of the angel's salutation. Then, too, both Zachary and the Blessed Virgin deliberate upon the angel's message. But in their deliberations we notice a difference. Zachary's hesitation is one of doubt, based merely upon a natural consideration of the words of the angel. In a purely human manner he wants a sign whereby he shall know that the prediction is true. For this incredulity he is punished by being struck dumb. The Blessed Virgin, on the other hand, does not doubt the words of the angel; but she has a grave and lofty reason to ask for an explanation before she gives her free consent. She knew that God did not ask her to break her vow of

---

[1]Meschler, *The Life of Our Lord*, Vol. I, p. 155.

virginity, yet He asked her to become the mother of His Son!
When the angel explained how this should be, she hesitated no
longer but humbly consented: "Be it done unto me according to
thy word."

4. *Was the announcement to the shepherds an announcement to
you also? How did the shepherds respond? And what is your
response?*

The announcement to the shepherds is also an announcement to
me and to you. The shepherds responded by leaving their night
watches at once and hastening "to see this word that is come to
pass, which the Lord hath showed to us." Our response should be
the same. We should detach ourselves from the things that will
perish in time and hasten to Christ and His eternal possessions.

5. *Why did Joseph and Mary go to Bethlehem to be enrolled?
Why is Christ sometimes called the Nazarene?*

Cæsar Augustus decreed that a universal census be taken.
Judea was also subject to Rome at this time, so the Jews were
obliged by the decree to enroll themselves as subjects of the em-
pire. But they had their own traditional method of taking an account of their population, by assembling themselves according to
the family and the tribe whence each had sprung. In this manner
they periodically revised the genealogical tables preserved in each
family city. Hence, when Cæsar decreed the census, the Jews
complied with the decree after their own fashion. Joseph, therefore, left his home at Nazareth and journeyed to Bethlehem to
enroll himself in the family city of David, who was his forefather.
Mary accompanied Joseph probably to appear as heiress of her
family at the enrolling, or perhaps to comply with a secret in-
spiration from heaven in order that Jesus might be born in Bethlehem according to the prophecy.

Christ is sometimes called the Nazarene because for thirty
years He lived in the town of Nazareth ("Nazara" from the
Hebrew "Nezer," meaning a shoot or a flower) where the home
of Mary and Joseph was. The word "Nazarene" as such (Vulgate,
"Nazaraeus") is found only once in the Gospels, that is, in Mat-

thew ii. 23. This one passage, however, seems to imply that our Lord was generally referred to as a Nazarene; that is, a native of Nazareth. (Cf. Matt. xxvi. 71; Mark i. 24, x. 47, xiv. 67; Luke iv. 34; John xviii. 5; and Acts ii. 22, where "Jesus Nazarenus" is rendered "Jesus of Nazareth" in our English Bibles.)

6. *What thoughts are suggested by the fact that Joseph and Mary could find no place in an inn, and Christ was born in a stable?*

It shows us Christ's love of humility, of poverty, and of a lowly hidden life. He who is the Lord and Master of all the riches of heaven and of earth chose a poor, humble life while on earth to show us the true way to heaven. He could have chosen to be born a prince in a palace and to have all the honors and comforts that earthly wealth provides. But no, He chose otherwise. In this we can see how our Lord esteems humility and poverty, and what He wishes us to do in order that we may merit the eternal riches of heaven.

7. *Show how each of the Messianic prophecies are fulfilled in Christ.*

(Cf. texts given in **14.** q. 1, pp. 65, 66.)

Genesis iii. 15: Christ overcame and crushed Satan, the enemy of man's salvation.

Genesis xxii. 18: All the nations of the earth are blessed in Christ because He has fulfilled the will of His Father by coming upon earth and redeeming all.

Micheas v. 2: Christ, the King of kings, was born at Bethlehem as has been prophesied.

Isaias vii. 14: Mary, who remained forever a virgin, conceived by the Holy Ghost and bore Jesus, the Second Person of the Blessed Trinity, who is truly the Emmanuel, God with us.

Psalm ii. 7: Jesus Himself declared that He is the Son of God and equal to the Father. "And the high priest said to Him: I adjure Thee by the living God, that Thou tell us if Thou be the Christ the Son of God. Jesus saith to him: Thou hast said it" (Matt. xxvi. 63–64). "I and the Father are one" (John x. 30).

Isaias ix. 6: Our Lord, and He alone, has merited the titles which the prophet here enumerates.

Psalm cix. 4: Christ was made a Priest by an oath, and shall remain forever the great High Priest of the New Law.

Psalm xxi. 19: The fulfillment of this prophecy is recorded in Matt. xxvii. 35.

Isaias liii. 5, 10: All these prophecies were fulfilled in our Lord's passion and death.

8. *What is the exact year of the birth of Christ?*

According to some historians the exact year of the birth of Christ was the year 5 B.C., or the 749th year after the founding of Rome. (So Fouard.) Others say it was 6 or 7 B.C., or the 748th or 747th year after the founding of Rome.

16.

THE EARLY LIFE OF CHRIST

Problem Questions, Chap. XVII, p. 135.

1. *What are the principal events in the first twenty-nine years of Christ's life?*

The principal events in the first twenty-nine years of Christ's life are:

a) His birth at Bethlehem.

b) His presentation in the Temple.

c) The visit of the Wise Men (the Magi).

d) The flight into Egypt and the return to Nazareth.

e) His journey to Jerusalem and stay in the Temple among the doctors at the age of twelve years.

2. *So far as you can find out, is there as good proof for these facts as there is for other facts (e.g., about Cæsar Augustus) of the same time?*

The historical documents we have to prove these facts are, to say the least, just as trustworthy as any others that have come down to us from that period.

3. *Name (give artist's name) or find a great picture illustrating each of the events in the early life of Christ.*

Heinrich Hoffmann (1824–1902), Bernhard Plockhorst (1825–1895), Michel Corneille (1642–1708), and Joseph Jansenns (contemporary) have made beautiful paintings illustrating each of the events in the early life of Christ.

4. *What does "Anno Domini" mean? What is the abbreviation for this?*

Anno Domini means "In the year of our Lord"; that is, in a specified year of the Christian Era. The abbreviation for this is "A.D."

5. *What was the statement by Simeon when Christ was presented in the Temple? What is meant by "presentation"? Who was Simeon?*

"And Simeon blessed them, and said to Mary, His mother: Behold this Child is set for the fall, and for the resurrection of many in Israel, and for a sign which shall be contradicted; and thy own soul a sword shall pierce, that, out of many hearts, thoughts may be revealed" (Luke ii. 34–35). "Presentation" means the bringing of the firstborn male child to the Temple and consecrating him to God according to the law stated in Exodus xiii. 2, and in Numbers iii. 13. Simeon was a distinguished and holy man residing in Jerusalem. Father Fouard says that perhaps he was the famous scribe Rabban Simeon, son of Hillel.

6. *When was Simeon's prophecy fulfilled?*

The prophecy of Simeon was fulfilled during the three years of Christ's public ministry and particularly on Good Friday.

7. *What statement was made by Anna, the prophetess?*

"Now she, at the same hour, coming in, confessed to the Lord; and spoke of Him to all that looked for the redemption of Israel" (Luke ii. 38).

8. *Show Heaven's guardianship of Christ during His early years.*

The Wise Men were advised in their sleep not to return to Herod after they had seen the Infant Christ. In this manner Herod failed to learn where Jesus lived (Matt. ii. 12).

Again Joseph received a command from heaven to take the Child and His mother into Egypt, so that when Herod caused all the boy children under two years to be put to death, Jesus again escaped his cruel designs (Matt. ii. 13–16).

Afterwards an angel told Joseph about Herod's death and bade him return to the land of Israel. Moreover, he warned Joseph to go to Galilee, lest the new ruler of Jerusalem, Archelaus, should endanger the life of our Lord (Matt. ii. 19–20, 22).

9. *Make a list of the appearances of angels in connection with the coming of Christ and His early life.*

a) The Angel Gabriel announced to Mary that she would become the mother of Jesus (Luke i. 26–38).

b) An angel appeared to Joseph, telling him that his espoused wife Mary would conceive by the Holy Ghost and give birth to Jesus (Matt. i. 20–21).

c) Angels appeared to the shepherds near Bethlehem and announced the birth of Christ (Luke ii. 9, 13).

d) An angel appeared to Joseph and told him to take his family to Egypt (Matt. ii. 13).

e) When Herod was dead, an angel again appeared to Joseph, telling him to return to Palestine (Matt. ii. 19–22).

10. *Describe the baptism of Christ by John in the River Jordan.*

"Then cometh Jesus from Galilee to the Jordan, unto John, to be baptized by him. But John stayed Him, saying: I ought to be baptized by Thee, and comest Thou to me? And Jesus answering, said to him: Suffer it to be so now. For so it becometh us to fulfill all justice. Then he suffered Him. And Jesus being baptized, forthwith came out of the water: and lo, the heavens were opened to Him: and He saw the Spirit of God descending as a dove, and coming upon Him. And behold a voice from heaven, saying: This is My beloved Son, in whom I am well pleased" (Matt. iii. 13–17. Also Luke iii. 21–22, and Mark i. 9–11).

11. *What significance have these facts with reference to the doctrine of the Trinity?*

In these facts the Trinity was made manifest to men for the first time. God the Father appeared in the Voice coming from the heavens; this Voice testified that Jesus, standing there, is God the Son; and resting over Jesus in the form of a Dove was God the Holy Ghost.

12. What is the doctrine of the Trinity? When was it first revealed to men?

The doctrine of the Trinity is that there is but one God in whom there are three distinct Persons: Father, Son, and Holy Ghost. These three Persons are equal in all things and possess one and the same divine nature and substance, being therefore one and the same God. This doctrine, although foreshadowed in the Old Testament, was first revealed to men at the baptism of Christ in the River Jordan.

13. What relation have the joyful mysteries of the Rosary to the childhood of Christ? What sorrows of Mary have relation to the childhood of Christ?

The joyful mysteries of the Rosary recall the facts about the childhood of Christ.

The sorrows of Mary which have relation to the childhood of Christ are those at the prophecy of Simeon, at the flight into Egypt, and at having lost the Holy Child in Jerusalem.

14. Why is Joseph called the foster father of Jesus?

Joseph is called the foster father of Jesus because he protected Him and His mother, took care of them, and supplied all the needs for the Holy Family. He was not, however, the real father of Christ — only a legal head of the Holy Family — and hence is called only a "foster" father of Jesus.

17.

THE DIVINITY OF CHRIST: THE MIRACLES

Problem Questions, Chap. XVIII, p. 143.

1. What is a miracle?

A miracle is an extraordinary event, perceptible to the senses, which exceeds the known powers of nature and can be traced to a divine cause.

2. *Make a list of the miracles performed by Christ according to the Gospels of St. Matthew, St. Luke, St. Mark, St. John. Describe two not given in this book.*

A list of the miracles performed by Christ according to the four Gospels:

St. Matthew

1) viii. 2–4: Cleansing of a leper (Mark i. 40–45; Luke v. 12–15).

2) viii. 5–13: Healing the centurion's servant (Luke vii. 2–10).

3) viii. 14–15: Curing Peter's mother-in-law (Mark i. 30–31; Luke iv. 38–39).

4) viii. 23–27: Calming the storm (Mark iv. 37–40; Luke viii. 23–25).

5) viii. 28–34: Healing two possessed Gerasens (Mark v. 2–20; Luke viii. 26–40).

6) ix. 2–8: Curing a man sick of the palsy (Mark ii. 3–12; Luke v. 18–26).

7) ix. 18–19, 23–26: Raising the daughter of Jairus (Mark v. 22–24, 35–43; Luke viii. 41–42, 49–56).

8) ix. 20–22: Healing the woman with issue of blood (Mark v. 25–34; Luke viii. 43–48).

9) ix. 27–31: Curing two blind men.

10) ix. 32–34: Healing a possessed dumb man (Luke xi. 14).

11) xii. 9–13: Healing the man with a withered hand (Mark iii. 1–5; Luke vi. 6–10).

12) xii. 22: Healing a blind and dumb demoniac.

13) xiv. 13–21: Feeding 5,000 men with five loaves and two fishes (Mark vi. 31–44; Luke ix. 10–17; John vi. 1–14).

14) xiv. 25–33: Walking on the Sea (Mark vi. 48–51; John vi. 19–21).

15) xv. 22–28: Healing the daughter of a Canaanite woman (Mark vii. 25–30).

16) xv. 32–39: Feeding 4,000 men with seven loaves and a few fishes (Mark viii. 1–9).

17) xvii. 14–20: Healing a possessed boy (Mark ix. 16–28; Luke ix. 38–43).

18) xvii. 26: The stater in a fish's mouth.

19) xx. 30–34: Healing two blind men (Mark x. 46–52; Luke xviii. 35–43).

20) xxi. 18–21: Withering of the barren fig tree (Mark xi. 13–14, 20).

21) iv. 23: Healing all manner of sickness and infirmity.

22) viii. 16: Casting out devils and healing the sick (Mark i. 32–34; Luke iv. 40–41).

23) xiv. 36: Healing many.

24) xv. 30: Healing the dumb, the blind, the lame, and the maimed.

St. Mark

25) i. 23–28: Healing a demoniac (Luke iv. 33–37).

26) vii. 32–35: Healing the deaf-and-dumb man.

27) viii. 22–26: Healing a blind man.

St. Luke

28) v. 1–11: The miraculous draught of fishes.

29) vii. 11–16: Raising the son of the widow of Naim.

30) xiii. 11–14: Healing a woman infirm for eighteen years.

31) xiv. 1–4: Curing the dropsical man.

32) xvii. 12–19: Cleansing ten lepers.

33) xxii. 49–51: Healing Malchus' ear.

34) vi. 18–19: Healing many.

St. John

35) ii. 1–11: Changing water into wine.

36) iv. 46–54: Curing the ruler's son.

37) v. 1–16: Healing the man at the Probatica pool.

38) ix. 1–34: Healing the man born blind.

39) xi. 1–45: Raising Lazarus to life.

40) xxi. 6–12: Second miraculous draught of fishes.

Raising the daughter of Jairus to life (Matt. ix. 18–19, 23–26).

"As He was speaking these things unto them, behold a certain ruler came up, and adored Him, saying: Lord, my daughter is even now dead; but come, lay Thy hand upon her, and she shall live.

"And Jesus, rising up, followed him with His disciples.

"And when Jesus was come into the house of the ruler, and saw the minstrels and the multitude making a rout, he said: Give place, for the girl is not dead, but sleepeth. And they laughed Him to scorn.

"And when the multitude was put forth, He went in, and took her by the hand. And the maid arose.

"And the fame hereof went abroad into all that country."

The Miraculous Draught of Fishes (Luke v. 4–9)

"Now when He had ceased to speak, He said to Simon: Launch out into the deep, and let down your nets for a draught.

"And Simon answering said to Him: Master, we have labored all the night, and have taken nothing: but at Thy word I will let down the net.

"And when they had done this, they enclosed a very great multitude of fishes, and their net broke.

"And they beckoned to their partners that were in the other ship, that they should come and help them. And they came, and filled both ships, so that they were almost sinking.

"Which when Simon Peter saw, he fell down at Jesus' knees, saying: Depart from me, for I am a sinful man, O Lord.

"For he was wholly astonished, and all that were with him, at the draught of the fishes which they had taken."

3. *Is Christ God because He performed the miracles, or did He perform the miracles because He is God?*

Christ performed the miracles because He is God.

4. *When was the statement made, "Surely this is the Son of God"? By whom?*

The statement was made by the centurion at the foot of the cross on Calvary, when he saw the earth quaking and the rocks splitting at the time of Christ's death (Matt. xxvii. 54; Mark xv. 39).

5. *Is there any other explanation of Christ's power except that He is God?*

There is no other explanation of Christ's power except that He is God.

18.

THE PUBLIC LIFE OF CHRIST: THE PARABLES

Problem Questions, Chap. XIX, p. 152.

1. *What is a parable?*

a) "A parable is a narration of some real or imaginary event which is intended to be interpreted with a heavenly meaning" (*Scripture Manuals,* Madame Cecelia).

b) "A parable is a short story in which a certain likeness makes clear the lesson one wishes to teach" (*Parables of the Gospel,* Fonck).

c) "As used in the Gospels, the word parable means a narrative of more or less fictitious character, but dealing with objects or occurrences taken from nature or the life of man, which serve as terms of comparison to illustrate a supernatural truth of the moral, religious order. In this narrative the expressions are to be understood in their ordinary sense, the words keeping their natural literal sense" (*Catholic Dictionary*).

d) "A parable is the illustration of a supernatural truth by means of a simile given in a complete self-dependent discourse" (William's *Textual Concordance*).

2. *Make a list of the parables given in the Gospel according to St. Matthew, St. Mark, St. Luke, St. John. Describe three parables not given in this book.*
Parables
(For significance of numbers in parentheses see next question.)

St. Matthew

1) Cockle and the Seed, xiii. 24–50.	(1)
2) Ungrateful Debtor, xviii. 23 ff.	(2)
3) Ungrateful Husbandmen, xxi. 33 ff.	(1)
4) Laborers in the Vineyard, xx. 1 ff.	(1)
5) The Leaven, xiii. 33.	(1)
6) The Marriage Feast, xxii. 1 ff.	(1)

7) The Mustard Seed, xiii. 31 ff.   (1)
8) Net Cast into Sea, xiii. 47 ff.   (1)
9) Pearl of Great Price, xiii. 45 ff.   (2)
10) Good and Bad Servants, xxiv. 44 ff.   (2)
11) Lost Sheep, xviii. 12.   (3)
12) The Two Sons, xxi. 28.   (1)
13) Sower and the Seed, xiii. 3–8.   (1)
14) The Talents, xxv. 14–30.   (2)
15) Treasure Hidden in a Field, xiii. 44.   (1)
16) Wise and Foolish Virgins, xxv. 1–13.   (2)
17) Bridegroom and Guests, ix. 15.   (1)
18) Children in Market-Place, xi. 16.   (1)
19) Divided Kingdom, xii. 25.   (1)
20) Fig Tree, xxiv. 32.   (1)
21) Narrow Gate, vii. 13.   (1)
22) House Built on a Rock, vii. 24.   (2)
23) The House Holder, xiii. 52.   (2)
24) Mote and Beam, vii. 3–5.   (2)
25) New Wine in Old Bottles, ix. 17.   (1)
26) Raw Cloth and New Garment, ix. 16.   (1)
27) Blind leading Blind, xv. 14.   (1)

St. Mark

1) Ungrateful Husbandmen, xii. 1 ff.   (1)
2) Mustard Seed, iv. 30.   (1)
3) Seed Cast into the Earth, iv. 26.   (1)
4) Good and Bad Servants, xiii. 34.   (2)
5) Sower and the Seed, iv. 2–8.   (1)
6) Bridegroom and Guests, ii. 18.   (1)
7) Divided Kingdom, iii. 23.   (1)
8) Fig Tree, xiii. 28.   (1)
9) New Wine in Old Bottles, ii. 22.   (1)
10) New Cloth in Old Garments, ii. 21.   (1)

St. Luke

1) Blind Leading the Blind, vi. 39.   (1)
2) Divided Kingdom, xi. 17–18.   (1)

3) Fig Tree, xxi. 29. (1)
4) Friend at Midnight, xi. 5. (2)
5) Narrow Gate, xiii. 24. (1)
6) House Built on a Rock, vi. 48. (2)
7) King about to War, xiv. 31. (2)
8) Mote and Beam, vi. 41. (2)
9) New Wine in Old Bottles, v. 37. (1)
10) New Cloth in Old Garments, v. 36. (1)
11) Building a Tower, xiv. 28. (2)
12) Forgiven Debtor, vii. 40 ff. (2)
13) Barren Fig Tree, xiii. 6 ff. (2)
14) Lost Groat, xv. 8 ff. (3)
15) Ungrateful Husbandmen, xx. 9 ff. (1)
16) Judge and the Widow, xviii. 1. (2)
17) The Leaven, xiii. 20 ff. (1)
18) The Mustard Seed, xiii. 18 ff. (1)
19) Pharisee and Publican, xviii. 9 ff. (2)
20) The Pounds, xix. 11 ff. (2)
21) The Prodigal Son, xv. 11 ff. (3)
22) Rich Man and Lazarus, xvi. 19 ff. (2)
23) Foolish Rich Man, xii. 16. (2)
24) Good Samaritan, x. 30. (2)
25) Good and Bad Servant, xii. 35. (2)
26) Lost Sheep, xv. 4. (3)
27) Sower and the Seed, viii. 4–15. (1)
28) The Unjust Steward, xvi. 1–8. (2)
29) The Great Supper, xiv. 16–24. (1)
30) Bridegroom and Guests, v. 33. (1)
31) Last Place at Feast, xiv. 7. (2)

St. John

1) The True Shepherd, x. 1–6. (3)
2) The Good Shepherd, x. 11–15. (3)
3) Light of the World, ix. 5. (3)
4) The True Vine, xv. 1. (3)
5) Woman in Labor, xvi. 21. (2)

References:

L. Fonck, *Parables of the Gospels* (New York: F. Pustet & Co., 1914), (for entire lesson).

T. W. Williams, *Textual Concordance of the Holy Scriptures* (New York: Benziger Bros., 1908).

Catholic Scripture Manuals — by Madame Cecilia (London: Burns, Oates and Washbourne, 1923).

Scripture Manuals for Catholic Schools, Ed. S. F. Smith, S.J. (London: Burns, Oates and Washbourne, Ltd.).

Parable of Friend at Midnight (Perseverance in Prayer)

"And He said to them: Which of you shall have a friend and shall go to him at midnight and shall say to him: Friend, lend me three loaves,

"Because a friend of mine is come off his journey to me and I have not what to set before him.

"And he from within should answer and say: Trouble me not; the door is now shut and my children are with me in bed; I cannot rise and give thee.

"Yet if he shall continue knocking, I say to you, although he will not rise and give him, because he is his friend; yet because of his importunity he will rise, and give him as many as he needeth" (Luke xi. 5–8).

Parable of the Rich Fool

"And He spoke a similitude to them saying: The land of a certain rich man brought forth plenty of fruits.

"And he thought within himself saying: What shall I do because I have no room where to bestow my fruits?

"And he said: This will I do: I will pull down my barns and will build greater: and into them will I gather all things that are grown to me, and my goods.

"And I will say to my soul: Soul, thou hast much goods laid up for many years, take thy rest, eat, drink, make good cheer.

"But God said to him: Thou fool, this night do they require thy soul of thee: And whose shall those things be which thou hast provided?" (Luke xii. 16–20.)

Parable of the Bridegroom and Guests

"And Jesus saith to them: Can the children of the marriage

fast as long as the bridegroom is with them? As long as they have the bridegroom with them they cannot fast.

"But the days will come when the bridegroom shall be taken away from them; and then they shall fast in those days" (Mark ii. 19, 20).

3. *Classify your list of parables by marking "1" after those parables which describe the kingdom of God, "2" after those parables which tell what must be done by members of the kingdom, and "3" after those parables which describe the head of the kingdom. (The teacher will consult Fonck's "The Parables of Christ").*

The parables are classified as directed by (1), (2), (3). See the preceding.

4. *Rewrite your list now, putting those three lists with the 1's together, the 2's together, and the 3's together. Give each list an appropriate title.*

(1) Kingdom of God
The Catholic Church

1. The Sower.
2. The Seed Cast into the Ground.
3. The Tares or Cockle.
4. The Mustard Seed.
5. The Leaven.
6. The Hidden Treasure.
7. The Pearl of Great Price.
8. The Fishing Net.
9. Great Harvest and Few Laborers.
10. Bridegroom and the Guests.
11. The Old Garment and the Old Bottles.
12. Old and New Wine.
13. Wayward Children.
14. Laborers in the Vineyard.
15. The Two Sons.
16. The Wicked Husbandmen.

17. Real Defilement.
18. Marriage of the King's Son.
19. The Great Supper.

(2) Members of the Kingdom
Duties of Catholics

1. Barren Fig Tree.
2. Good Tree and the Bad.
3. Pharisee and the Publican.
4. The Last Place at the Feast.
5. The Rich Fool.
6. Vigilant Servants.
7. The Thief in the Night.
8. Faithful Steward.
9. The Ten Virgins.
10. The Five Talents.
11. The Pounds.
12. Unprofitable Servants.
13. Good Samaritan.
14. Unjust Steward.
15. Rich Man and Lazarus.
16. The Unmerciful Servant.
17. Mote and the Beam.
18. Friend at Midnight.
19. Unjust Judge.
20. The Two Debtors.
21. King Going to War.
22. House Built on a Rock.

(3) Head of the Kingdom
Qualities of Christ

1. Light of the World.
2. The Vine.
3. The Prodigal Son.
4. The Good Shepherd.
5. The Lost Sheep.
6. The Lost Coin.

5. *What is your duty, according to the parables, as a member of the Kingdom of God?*

The duties we have as members of the Kingdom of God, according to the Parables, are:[1]

1) Practice humility.
2) Have confidence in God.
3) Pray sincerely and constantly.
4) Practice charity toward our neighbor (all people).
5) Love God.
6) Forgive injuries.
7) Watch and pray.
8) Make good use of riches.
9) Be just to all.
10) Be prudent.

6. *What qualities of the parables made them easy to understand?*

Parables were easy to understand because therein "Christ spoke of the highest and most far-reaching truths in terms of the vital daily experience of His listeners." Hence we may list the following qualities:[2]

1) Simplicity.
2) Brevity.
3) Concreteness.
4) Use of commonplace objects for comparisons.
5) Things and events on which the parables are based fall within the experience of all men.

7. *Why, then, do you think more of the Jews did not become followers of Christ?*

The evil disposition of the Jews prevented them from following Christ in great numbers. This term (evil disposition) would include:

1) Pride.
2) Materialism.

---

[1] Cf. Fonck, *Parables of Our Lord*, p. 26 ff.
[2] Cf. Bandas, *Catechetical Methods.*

3) Envy.

4) Externalization of worship.

5) Spiritual blindness.

6) Misconception (obdurate) of the Messiah and of His Kingdom.

19.

SOME MEMORABLE SAYINGS OF CHRIST

Problem Questions, Chap. XX, p. 159.

1. *Quote the Beatitudes.*

The Beatitudes:

1) Blessed are the poor in spirit: for theirs is the kingdom of Heaven.

2) Blessed are the meek: for they shall possess the land.

3) Blessed are they that mourn: for they shall be comforted.

4) Blessed are they that hunger and thirst after justice: for they shall have their fill.

5) Blessed are the merciful: for they shall obtain mercy.

6) Blessed are the clean of heart: for they shall see God.

7) Blessed are the peacemakers: for they shall be called the children of God.

8) Blessed are they that suffer persecution for justice' sake: for theirs is the kingdom of heaven (Matt. v. 3–12).

2. *What is meant by "Beatitude"?*

Definitions of Beatitude:

1) By "Beatitude" we mean that "declaration made in the Sermon on the Mount (Matt. v. 3–12) with regard to the blessedness of those having specified virtues" (*Webster's Dictionary*).

2) The declarations "are called 'Beatitudes' because they tell us the way to blessedness" (cf. page 154 of Text).

3) By "beatitudes" we mean "the blessings pronounced in the opening words of the Sermon on the Mount." (*Catholic Dictionary.*)

3. What is regarded as Christ's greatest address? Can you quote any part of it besides the Beatitudes?

The Sermon on the Mount. There are many sections that may be quoted as:

1) Matt. v. 13–16:

"You are the salt of the earth. But if the salt lose its savor wherewith shall it be salted? It is good for nothing any more but to be cast out and to be trodden on by men."

"You are the light of the world. A city seated on a mountain cannot be hid."

"So let your light shine before men that they may see your good works and glorify your Father who is in heaven."

2) Matt. v. 48:

"Be ye therefore perfect as your heavenly Father is perfect."

3) Matt. vi. 25, 26:

"Therefore I say to you, be not solicitous for your life what you shall eat, nor for your body what you shall put on. Is not the life more than the meat? and the body more than the raiment? Behold the birds of the air, for they neither sow, nor do they reap, nor gather in their barns and your heavenly Father feedeth them. Are not you of much more value than they?"

4) Other sections that might be quoted are: v. 21–24; vi. 5, 6; vi. 8–15.

4. Quote any statement of Christ about children. Can you quote one not given in this book?

The following may be quoted:

1) Mark x. 13, 14:

"And they brought to Him young children that He may touch them. And the disciples rebuked them that brought them. Whom when Jesus saw, was much displeased and saith to them: Suffer little children to come unto Me and forbid them not: for of such is the kingdom of God."

2) Mark ix. 35, 36:

"And taking a child, He set him in the midst of them. Whom when He had embraced, He saith to them: Whosoever shall receive one such child as this in My name receiveth Me. And who-

soever shall receive Me, receiveth not Me, but Him who sent
Me."

5. *What were Christ's answers to the following questions:*
   1) Matt. xix. 16–24.
   "But if thou wilt enter into life keep the commandments. He
said to Him: Which? and Jesus said: thou shalt do no murder,
thou shalt not commit adultery, thou shalt not steal, thou shalt
not bear false witness. Honor thy father and thy mother and
thou shalt love they neighbor as thyself. The young man saith
to Him: all these have I kept from my youth, what is yet wanting to me? Jesus saith to him: If thou wilt be perfect, go sell
what thou hast and give it to the poor and thou shalt have
treasure in heaven: and come and follow Me."
   2) Matt. xxii. 38.
   "Thou shalt love the Lord thy God with thy whole heart and
with thy whole soul and with thy whole mind. This is the greatest
and the first commandment."
   3) Matt. xxii. 21.
   "Render therefore to Cæsar the things that are Cæsar's and to
God, the things that are God's."
   4) Matt. xvi. 26, 27.
   "For what doth it profit a man, if he gain the whole world and
suffer the loss of his own soul? or what exchange shall a man
give for his soul? For the Son of Man shall come in the glory of
His Father with His angels and then will He render to every man
according to his works."
   5) Luke x. 30–37.
   The entire parable of the Good Samaritan should be read here.
   Verse 37: "But he said: He that showed mercy to him."

a) What shall I do to gain everlasting life?
   Keep the commandments. Love God above all things and our
neighbor as ourselves for love of God. Sacrifice whatever is a
hindrance to our salvation, and give up all for Christ if we feel
ourselves called to a religious life.

b) Which is the greatest commandment?

We must love God above all else and with all our powers. This love must be translated into good works. It will also induce us to keep all of God's commands. "If you love Me, keep My commandments" (John xiv. 15), (cf. *St. Luke*, by Madame Cecelia).

c) Is it lawful to pay tribute to Cæsar (the state)?

"Man's first allegiance is due to his Creator. Therefore we are to obey the higher powers (governmental authorities) only when this obedience does not clash with the law of God. Then we must obey God rather than man" (cf. *St. Matthew*, by Madame Cecelia).

d) What shall a man give in exchange for his soul?

If we deliberately, at the expense of our salvation, seek riches and the pleasures of the world, what advantage will it be to us? For if we lose our soul, we lose all. Riches, pleasures, and enjoyments are as nothing compared to eternal beatitude. They will be of no help to us at the last judgment. Therefore, we must not barter heaven for a transitory (sinful) joy and pleasure or for a little money.

e) Who is my neighbor?

It is our duty to show Christian charity to each and every human being because we are all brothers and sisters in Christ.

6. What application to your own life is contained in answer to each of the foregoing questions?

20.

CHRIST AND THE HOLY EUCHARIST

Problem Questions, Chap. XXI, pp. 170, 172.

1. Trace the happenings of the last week of Christ's life, day by day, up to the Crucifixion.

The Last Week of Christ's Life.

Palm Sunday

    1) Christ's triumphant entry into Jerusalem.

    2) He goes to Bethany in the evening.

Monday

    1) Curses the fig tree on the way to Jerusalem.

    2) Drives the money changers from the Temple.

    3) He speaks to the Greeks.

Tuesday

    1) Christ speaks with the Sanhedrin delegation in the Temple.

    2) Tells the parable of the vineyard and the vine dressers.

    3) Tells the parable of the wedding feast.

    4) Cæsar's coin.

    5) Talks to the Sadducees about future life.

    6) Enunciates "the greatest commandment."

    7) Denounces the Pharisees.

    8) He weeps over the city of Jerusalem.

    9) Discourses on the widow's mite.

    10) Foretells the fall of Jerusalem and the destruction of the Temple.

    11) Describes the second coming.

    12) Propounds the parable of the Ten Virgins.

    13) Foretells His Passion and Death.

Wednesday

    1) Christ was not in the Temple nor in Jerusalem on this day. It is possible that He spent the day at Bethany.

Thursday (Holy)

    1) The Last Supper.

        a) He washes the feet of His Apostles.

        b) Institutes the Holy Eucharist and the priesthood.

        c) Foretells the fall of Peter.

        d) Delivers His last discourse to the Apostles. (Mention should be made here of the beautiful sacerdotal prayer of Christ, John xvii.)

    2) The agony in the garden.

    3) He is betrayed by Judas.

    4) Heals the ear of Malchus.

5) He is brought before Annas.

6) He is brought before Caiphas.

7) He is ill-treated and abused in the council room.

8) He is denied by Peter.

9) He is in the hands of Sanhedrin guards.

Friday (Good)

1) Christ before the Sanhedrin (at dawn).

2) Christ at the praetorium of Pilate.

3) Sent to Herod.

4) "Christ or Barabbas" and the cries of "Crucify Him."

5) He is scourged and crowned with thorns.

6) *Ecce Homo.*

7) He is delivered by Pilate to the Jews to be crucified.

8) The way of the cross:[1]

   a) Meeting with the Blessed Mother* (not narrated in the Gospels).

   b) Simon of Cyrene helps Jesus to carry the cross.

   c) Veronica wipes the face of Jesus* (not narrated in the Gospels).

   d) Women of Jerusalem weep over Him.

   e) The three falls* (not mentioned in the Gospels).

   f) He is stripped of His garments.

   g) He is crucified.

   h) The seven words.

   i) He dies.

2. *What was the Feast of the Pasch? When was it instituted? In memory of what happenings?*

The Feast of the Pasch was one of the three great annual religious feasts of the Jews. It was instituted by Moses at the command of God to commemorate the deliverance of the Jews from the bondage of Egypt. On the night before deliverance, the Jews sacrificed a lamb or a kid without spot or blemish, the bones of which were preserved unbroken. The blood of the lamb was

---

[1]This arrangement has been based on *The Christ: The Son of God:* a life of our Lord and Savior Jesus Christ, by the Abbé Constant Fouard. Abbé Fouard does not mention the incidents of the way of the cross that are followed by an asterisk.

then springled on the doorpost of every Hebrew house, so that when the destroying angel passed over Egypt to kill every first-born in the land, he passed over the houses marked by the lamb's blood, preserving the firstborn of that house. This feast was celebrated on the fourteenth of Nisan (March to April).

NOTE: Chapters twelve and thirteen of the Book of Exodus should be read in this connection. See also *The Catholic Dictionary* and *Catholic Scripture Manuals: St. John,* by Madame Cecelia (Burns, Oates & Washbourne).

3. *What did Christ think of the Jewish priests?*

Christ condemned the Jewish priests and Scribes because they had reduced the Jewish God-given religion into a mere formality — a matter of external ceremonies. But more than that, the Jewish priests had utterly failed to observe the laws of justice and charity and other precepts given by God Himself in the Decalogue. Their lives were a scandal to the people.

The following chapters should be read in this connection: St. Mark, chapters 11 and 12; St. Matthew, chapters 21 and 23; St. Luke, chapter 20.

However, the point must be emphasized that Christ respected the priesthood as such and its authority. It was the priests' mode of living that was condemned. For He said: "The Scribes and the Pharisees have sitten on the chair of Moses. All things therefore whatsoever they shall say to you observe and do: but according to their works do ye not." (See Matt. xxiii. 2, 4 ff.) Also confer *The Christ: The Son of God,* by Abbé Constant Fouard, Book VI, Chapter II, Part IV.

4. *Describe the events of Thursday evening.*

The Events of (Holy) Thursday Evening.

A) The Last Supper (the complete ceremony in schema).

    1) Lamb slaughtered and roasted during the day.

    2) At nightfall a number (10 to 20) of guests assembled.

    3) Ceremony began with a cup of wine, mingled with water, being passed around by the head of the family.

    4) A napkin and a basin of water passed around. (This is

probably the time when Christ washed the feet of His Apostles).

5) The bitter herbs, lamb, unleavened bread now on the table.

6) Second cup of wine passed around the table and the entire ceremony as well as symbolism of each thing and action explained to the younger members of the family.

7) Eating of the unleavened (azyme) bread "which was thin and tasteless like the paste which the yeast had not time to leaven before the flight of Israel." Here is where our Lord probably consecrated the Bread and said: "Do this in commemoration of Me."

8) Singing of the "Hallel" (Psalms 112 to 118, inclusive).

9) Eating of the lamb (once carved it must be entirely disposed of and no bones were to be broken).

10) The third cup of wine passed around (probably the one consecrated by Christ).

11) Final psalms of "Hallel."

12) The fourth cup was passed around.

13) Foretelling Peter's fall and the Commandment of Love.

14) On the way out of the Upper Room Christ utters His Last Discourse.

This discourse (John xiv, xv, xvi, and xvii) should be read to or by the pupils. Chapter xii may be included for its beauty.

B) The Agony in the Garden.[1]

1) Christ takes three disciples (Peter, James, and John) deep into the Garden of Gethsemani.

2) He prays to His Heavenly Father.

3) Finds the disciples sleeping . . . warns them to watch and pray.

4) Christ prays again: "My Father, if this chalice may not pass away but I must drink it, Thy will be done."

5) Finds the Apostles sleeping again.

---

[1]This arrangement is based upon *The Christ: The Son of God*, by Abbé Constant Fouard. The Gospels also have been consulted and should be read by the teacher in preparation of this lesson.

6) The comforting angel. Prays again and bloody sweat pours from His Limbs.

7) Returns to His Apostles just when the mob is come to arrest Him.

5. *What do we mean by the phrase "betrayed by a kiss"? Describe the events in Christ's life (beginning early Thursday evening) which gave rise to this expression.*

"Betrayed by a kiss."

The kiss was to serve a twofold purpose. First, in the East the kiss is a sign of friendship and a sign of respect. Judas thus wished to act as a faithful disciple and to conceal his treachery at least from the other Apostles. Secondly, many of those who were to arrest Jesus did not know Him personally. Also it was night when Jesus was taken and it would have been difficult to distinguish our Lord from one of the disciples. Therefore a sign from the traitor was needed.

The expression "betrayed by a kiss" was first used by our Lord Himself. We read in Luke xxii. 48: "And Jesus said to him: Judas, dost thou betray the Son of Man with a kiss?" The arrest of Jesus and His passion and death that followed (described in Question 1) imprinted the phrase on the souls of all Christians.

6. *Describe what happened in Christ's two appearances before Pontius Pilate.*

A) First appearance of Christ before Pilate[2] (Matt. xxvii. 11–26; Mark xv. 2–15; Luke xxiii. 1–5; John xviii. 28–40):

    1) Jesus accused of:

        a) Perverting the nation.

        b) Forbidding to give tribute to Cæsar.

        c) Saying that He is Christ the King.

    2) Jesus answers nothing to the charges. His only recorded words are "Thou sayest it" when Pilate asked Him "Art Thou the king of the Jews?" (Luke xxiii. 3.)

    3) Pilate declares our Lord innocent, whereupon the false witnesses again charge Him with sedition.

---

[2]This is taken from *Catholic Scripture Manuals,* see *St. Luke,* by Madame Cecelia, p. 206.

4) Pilate sends Jesus to Herod.

B) Second appearance of Christ before Pilate (Matt. xxvii. 15–26; Mark xv. 6–15; Luke xxiii. 13–25):

1) Pilate pronounces Jesus to be innocent.

2) He proposes to chastise Jesus and to release Him.

3) The people claim their privilege (of having one criminal released on the festival day) and Pilate offers to release Jesus.

4) Pilate receives his wife's message, "Have nothing to do with this just Man."

5) The chief priests urge the multitude to ask for the release of Barabbas.

6) Pilate again asserts Christ's innocence.

7) Pilate washes his hands as a proof of his own innocence.

8) Jesus is delivered up to be scourged.

9) Pilate once more asserts Christ's innocence.

10) He tries to move the people to pity, *Ecce Homo*.

11) The Sanhedrin now clamors for Christ's crucifixion.

12) Pilate once more bids them try Him themselves.

13) Pilate questions Jesus and seeks to release Him.

14) The Jews prevail on Pilate to yield by insinuating that to act otherwise would be an act of disloyalty.

15) Pilate pronounces the sentence of death against Jesus.

21.

THE CRUCIFIXION

Problem Questions, Chap. XXII, p. 181.

1. *Describe step by step the events on Friday after the condemnation of Christ.*

1) The cross is placed on Christ's shoulder.[1]

2) Christ falls under the cross (not mentioned in the Gospel).

3) Simon of Cyrene helps Jesus to carry the cross.

4) Jesus comforts the women who weep over Him.

---

[1]This arrangement is based on *The Christ: The Son of God*, by Fouard, and on *Synopsis Evangeliorum secundum Mattheum, Marcum et Lucam*, by Camerlynck.

5) The soldiers give Christ to drink wine mingled with gall (Matt. xxvii. 34). He tasted it but refused to drink.

6) Christ is stripped of His garments.

7) He is crucified (nailed to the cross).

8) Two thieves are crucified with Him, one on each side of Him.

9) The soldiers divide His garments by lot among themselves

10) Christ is mocked by the chief priests and the people.

11) Christ utters the seven words (see question 4).

12) Conversion of the "good" thief.

13) The darkness (unusual for the sixth hour) spreads over Calvary, over the city, and over the country.

14) A soldier fills a sponge with vinegar, puts it on a reed and gives Jesus to drink.

15) Jesus cries with a loud voice and dies.

16) The Temple veil is rent in two; the earth quakes; dead rise from the graves.

17) The centurion confesses that "indeed this was the Son of God."

18) One of the soldiers plunges his lance in His side and blood and water flow forth.

19) Nicodemus and Joseph of Arimathea take down from the cross the Body of our Lord.

20) The Body of Christ is anointed and wrapped in linen.

21) His Body is laid in the grave.

2. *What events are omitted in the devotions of the "stations"?*
Events omitted in the devotions of the "stations":

1) Giving Christ to drink wine mingled with gall.

2) The mocking of the chief priests and people.

3) The seven words.

4) The unnatural phenomena of darkness and rising of some who had been dead.

5) Conversion of the penitent thief.

6) Confession of the centurion.

7) Piercing of His side.

3. *Name the fourteen "stations."*

The fourteen "stations" are:

1) Jesus is condemned to death.
2) Jesus is laden with the cross.
3) Jesus falls the first time under His cross.
4) Jesus meets His afflicted Mother.
5) The Cyrenean helps Jesus to carry His cross.
6) Veronica wipes the Face of Jesus.
7) Jesus falls the second time.
8) Jesus speaks to the women of Jerusalem.
9) Jesus falls the third time.
10) Jesus is stripped of His garments.
11) Jesus is nailed to the cross.
12) Jesus dies on the cross.
13) Jesus is taken down from the cross.
14) Jesus is placed in the sepulcher.

4. *What statements of Christ on that first Good Friday are the basis of the devotion called the "Tre Ore"?*

The Last Words (statements) of Christ:

1) "Father forgive them: for they know not what they do."
2) "Amen, I say to thee, this day thou shalt be with Me in paradise."
3) "Woman, behold thy Son." "Behold thy Mother."
4) "My God, My God, why hast Thou forsaken Me?"
5) "I thirst."
6) "It is consummated."
7) "Father into Thy hands I commend My spirit."

5. *Why was the "good thief" admitted to heaven? What application is there in the incident of the good thief to our life?*

The answer to this question is taken from *Watches of the Passion,* by Gallwey, S.J., Vol. II, p. 329.

A. "In a moment, in the twinkling of an eye, as it were, the soul of the sinner has been wafted across the chaos that lay between him and his God, and, full of filial hope, draws near and says, Remember me, my God, my Father. Dysmas (the penitent thief) could not make his prayer unless the grateful Lord had already done great things for him. St. Thomas writes that it is a miracle (of moral order) when a sinner, without passing slowly through intermediate stages, is so strongly moved by grace that he suddenly arrives at the perfection of sanctity. Of his great faith St. John Chrysostom says: 'He sees Jesus a condemned man, but invokes Him as a King; sees Him on a cross, but prays to Him as if enthroned in Heaven.' He and other Fathers call St. Dysmas, 'Prophet, Apostle, Evangelist.' "

B. We should remember that no matter how much we have sinned in the past, a perfect act of contrition of love, that springs from lively faith, always brings down on us the unspeakable mercy of God.

6. What pictures of the crucifixion appeal especially to you? Why? Name the artists of these pictures.

The following pictures of the Crucifixion appeal on account of their artistic value and their capacity to inspire the soul with pious and holy thoughts and sentiments:

1) *Crucifixion,* by Guido Reni (1575–1642).
2) *Crucifixion,* by Fra Angelico (1387–1455).
3) *Crucifixion,* by Peter Rubens (1577–1640).
4) *Crucifixion,* by Gaudenzio Ferrari (1470–1546).
5) *Crucifixion,* by Bernardino Luini (1476–1533).

7. Has the crucifixion been treated often in literature? Why?

Suffering is the deepest and truest thing in our nature since the Fall. At the same time, it appeals most directly to our sympathies, as the very structure of language indicates. To go no further than our own, we have English words such as condolence to express sympathy with grief; but we have no one word to express sympathy with joy. Friendship is scarcely sure until it has been proved in suffering. But the chains of an affection riveted in that fiery furnace are not easily broken. Now, the Passion of Jesus was the greatest revelation of His sympathy and love for us in our misery: "Greater love hath no man than this, that a man lay down his life for his friends." Men's minds and hearts are knit closely to Christ because He chose the road of suffering. It is, indeed, no accidental peculiarity of the few, but a law of our present being which the poet's words express:

> That to the Cross the mourner's eye should turn,
> Sooner than where the stars of Christmas burn.

8. *What is meant by a Passion Play? Which is the most famous of the Passion Plays? Can you find out the history of the Passion Play?*

A. A Passion Play may be defined briefly as "a mystery play depicting the gospel story of the Passion of Our Lord" (*Webster's Dictionary*) and a Mystery Play in turn, is defined as "a religious drama which developed among Christian nations at the end of the Middle Ages" (*Catholic Encyclopedia*).

B. The most famous Passion Play today is the one held at Oberammergau. "The first mention we find of it is in 1633, when it is referred to in connection with a vow made to obtain relief from the Black Death, when the people of Ammergau vowed to produce the play every ten years. As early as 1634 the drama was enacted. Since this Passion Play was then well-known, productions must have taken place before that date. The oldest text still in existence was written about 1600. About the middle of the eighteenth century the text was revised by the Benedictine Rosner. In 1780 this bombastic version was again reduced to a simpler form by the Benedictine Krupfelberger. Finally, P. Otmar Weiss and M. Daiseberger gave it its present simple and dignified form and transcribed the verse into prose" (*Catholic Encyclopedia*).

C. The history of the Passion Play in a short outline:

1) Originated in the ritual of the Catholic Church. (Here one may confer the sung Gospel on Good Friday which is divided among several persons.)

2) First plays were in Latin and then in German (still based on the Gospel).

3) Plays only in German and conform to popular ideas (resembled oratorios in parts).

4) In the thirteenth century a rapid development ensued and

the famous "Vienna Passion," "St. Gall Passion," and others were enacted.

5) The highest point of development was reached at about the period 1400 to 1515. "Frankfurt Passion Play," the "Alsferder," and others are enacted.

6) Tyrol Plays became very elaborate about this period and served as sources to all others.

7) The decline of the plays into which were introduced worldly, coarse, and even sinful elements.

8) Gradual suppression of the plays by bishops and synods.

9) Carnivals and school dramas took their place.

10) Attempts to destroy even their remnants in the later part of the eighteenth and nineteenth century in Bavaria and Tyrol.

11) The revival of the plays in the nineteenth century in Tyrol, Southern Bohemia, and especially Bavaria.

12) The chief and most famous survival; the Passion Play at Oberammergau.

NOTE: Some sources on this topic should be consulted as:

(1) *Catholic Encyclopedia;* (2) Chambers, *The Medieval Stage,* Oxford, 1903; (3) Pollard, *English Miracle Plays,* London, 1904; (4) Froning, *Das Drama des Mittelalter,* Berlin (no date).

9. *What basis is there for the statement that "Christ descended into hell" (Limbo)?*

The statement that "Christ descended into hell" is based on:

1) Acts ii. 29–31:

"Ye men brethren let me freely speak to you of the patriarch David; That he died and was buried: and his sepulcher is with us to this present day.

"Whereas therefore he was a prophet and knew that God hath sworn to him with an oath that of the fruit of his loins one should sit upon his throne.

"Foreseeing this he spoke of the resurrection of Christ. For *neither was he left in hell, neither did his flesh see corruption.*

"This Jesus hath God raised again whereof all we are witnesses."

2) I Peter iii. 18–20:

"Because Christ also died once for our sins, the just for the unjust that He might offer us to God, being put to death indeed in the flesh but enlivened *in His spirit*.

"In which also coming He preached to those spirits that were in prison.

"Which had been sometime incredulous when they waited for the patience of God in the days of Noe when the ark was a building."

3) I Peter iv. 5–6:

"Who shall render account to Him who is ready to judge the living and the dead.

"For, for this cause *was the gospel preached also to the dead*: that they might be judged indeed according to men, in the flesh; but may live according to God, in the Spirit."

The term "hell" in these passages does not denote the place where those who die in the state of mortal sin are confined. By "hell" is meant the place where the just of the Old Testament were waiting, and expecting the opening of heaven by Christ. It must be remembered that in the history of Catholic theology any place lower than heaven was called "hell" (*infernum*).

22.

HE IS RISEN

Problem Questions, Chap. XXIII, p. 191.

1. *Describe the Resurrection.*

The Resurrection itself is not portrayed in the Gospels but only the accomplished fact. The disciples and the holy women and others see, touch, and talk to the risen Christ. St. Matthew gives us an account of what happened and with this we must be content.

St. Matthew's version (xxviii. 1–9):

"And in the end of the Sabbath, when it began to dawn toward the first day of the week, came Mary Magdalen and the other Mary to see the sepulcher.

"And behold there was a great earthquake. For an angel of the Lord descended from heaven and coming rolled back the stone and sat upon it.

"And his countenance was as lightning and his raiment as snow. And for fear of him the guards were struck with terror and became as dead men.

"And the angel answering said to the women: Fear not you: for I know that you seek Jesus who was crucified.

"He is not here, for He is risen as He said. Come and see the place where the Lord was laid."

2. Describe the Ascension.

The Ascension is recorded by St. Luke in the Acts of the Apostles (i. 9–11) in the following terms:

"And when He had said these things while they looked on, He was raised up: and a cloud received Him out of their sight.

"And while they were beholding Him going up to heaven, behold two men stood by them in white garments.

"Who also said: Ye men of Galilee why stand you looking up to heaven? This Jesus who is taken up from you into heaven shall so come as you have seen Him going into heaven."

3. Why is the Resurrection the most important event of Christ's life on earth?

"The Resurrection shows that Christ is God. When the Jews pressed our Lord on the question of His Divinity, when they demanded a proof or a sign of His divine mission, He, to convince their mind and confound their incredulity, always referred them to His future Resurrection. This wicked and incredulous generation, He once said of the Jews, wishes to be assured by a miracle as to who I am, but it shall have no other miracle except that of which Jonas was the figure: 'Destroy this temple and in three days I shall raise it up.' If Christ after His death had not risen, belief in His divinity would have been destroyed by the word of His mouth: His divinity destroyed, His other miracles would lose their force, His words would become a falsehood, and Christian faith a phantom. But if after this

23.

MARY, FULL OF GRACE

Problem Questions, Chap. XXIV, p. 201.

1. *Describe two Madonnas you like, and tell why.*

The two Madonnas that might be suggested are:

1) *The Madonna of the Chair,* by Raphael (1483–1521).

"The whole of maternal love seems to be enclosed within the perfect circle of this picture. . . . In it the most ordinary human life reaches its noblest expression, a universal beauty."[1]

2) *The Sistine Madonna,* by Raphael (1483–1521).

"When one looks at the face of the Virgin, he seems no longer to be gazing at a picture but to behold a heavenly vision. . . . That lovely countenance, so full of feeling and sweetness, those wonderful eyes, which seem always to gaze on the beholder, appears to live and one waits with breathless awe to hear the Virgin speak."[2]

2. *Name and describe five great paintings of events of Mary's life. Name the artist.*

1) *Immaculate Conception,* by Bartolome Murillo (1617–1682).

2) *Coronation,* by Fra Angelico (1387–1455).

3) *Assumption,* by Titian (1477–1577).

4) *Sorrowful Mother,* by Bartolome Murillo (1617–1682).

5) *Pieta,* by Fra Bartolommeo (1475–1517).

6) *The Annunciation,* by Leonardo da Vinci (1452–1519).

---

[1]E. F. Garesché, S.J., *Great Christian Artists* (Milwaukee: Bruce Publishing Company, 1924), p. 52.
[2]*Op. cit.,* p. 57.

3. *Write a brief biography of Mary's life.*

Brief outline of the Life of Blessed Virgin Mary:

1) Immaculate Conception (Dogma of the Church).

2) Nativity of Mary (probably at Nazareth) the daughter of Joachim and Anna (Patristic tradition).

3) The name of Mary is bestowed upon her.

4) Presentation of Mary at the Temple (probably at the age of six), (Liturgy — Feast of the Presentation of Mary — November 21).

5) Espousal to St. Joseph (Luke i. 27).

6) Annunciation (Luke i. 26–38).

7) Visitation (Luke i. 39–56).

8) Marriage to St. Joseph (Matt. i. 24).

9) Nativity of our Lord (Luke ii. 7).

10) Presentation of our Lord in the Temple and the prophecy of Simeon (Luke ii. 22–35). Also called Purification or Candlemas Day.

11) Exile in Egypt (Matt. ii. 13–15).

12) Private life at Nazareth (Matt. ii. 19–23).

13) The Loss and Finding of the Child Jesus (Luke ii. 41–52).

14) Public life of Christ (Gospel does not say if Mary accompanied Him as one of the holy women. However, we know that she was with Him on some occasions, as at the wedding in Cana) (John ii. 1–11).

15) Meeting of Jesus on His way to Calvary (Tradition — the fourth station).

16) Beneath the cross (John xix. 25).

17) Jesus is taken down from the cross and placed in the arms of His Mother (Tradition — the thirteenth station).

18) The Resurrection and first appearance to Mary (Tradition).

19) Living at the house of St. John (John xix. 27).

20) In the Cenacle on Pentecost Day (Acts i. 14).

21) Her death either at Jerusalem or Ephesus (Tradition).

22) Her Assumption (equivalently a dogma of the Church as it is believed by the universal Church).

NOTE: This arrangement is based (1) on the Gospels; (2) on the Missal and Church Liturgy; (3) on *Life of the Blessed Virgin,* by Rev. B. Rohner, O.S.B. (New York: Benziger Bros., 1897.)

4. *Quote the Magnificat.*

The *Magnificat* (Luke i. 46–55):

My soul doth magnify the Lord.

And my spirit hath rejoiced in God my Savior.

Because He hath regarded the humility of His handmaid: for behold from henceforth all generations shall call me blessed.

Because He that is mighty hath done great things to me and holy is His name.

And His mercy is from generation unto generations, to them that fear Him.

He hath showed might in His arm: He hath scattered the proud in the conceit of their heart.

He hath put down the mighty from their seat, and hath exalted the humble.

He hath filled the hungry with good things: and the rich He hath sent empty away.

He hath received Israel His servant, being mindful of His mercy.

As He spoke to our fathers, to Abraham and to his seed forever.

5. *What are the great feast days of Mary? Are any of them holydays of obligation?*

The great feasts of Mary:

1) Assumption (Aug. 15) holyday of obligation.
2) Immaculate Conception (Dec. 8) holyday of obligation.
3) Purification (Feb. 2).
4) Annunciation (March 25).
5) Nativity of Mary (Sept. 8).
6) Name of Mary (Sept. 12).

7) Seven Sorrows (Sept. 15).
8) Holy Rosary of B.V.M. (Oct. 7).
9) Presentation (Nov. 21).

6. *Name the mysteries of the Holy Rosary. Are they a summary of Mary's life?*
The mysteries of the Rosary:

A. *Joyful Mysteries*   *Sorrowful Mysteries*   *Glorious Mysteries*

1) Annunciation	1) Agony in the garden	1) Resurrection
2) Visitation		2) Ascension
3) Nativity	2) Scourging at the pillar	3) Descent of the Holy Ghost
4) Presentation	3) Crowning with thorns	4) Assumption of B.V.M.
5) Finding of the Child Jesus in the Temple	4) Carrying of the cross	5) Coronation of B. V. M. in heaven
	5) Crucifixion	

B. In a way, the mysteries of the Rosary are a summary of Mary's life as they show the outstanding events in her life.

7. *What are the "Sorrows of Mary"?*
The "Sorrows of Mary" are:
1) The prophecy of Simeon.
2) The flight into Egypt.
3) The loss of the Child Jesus when He was twelve years old.
4) The meeting with Jesus on the way of the cross.
5) Witnessing the suffering and death of her Divine Son.
6) The taking down from the cross of the Body of Jesus and laying It in her arms.
7) The placing of the Body of Jesus in the sepulcher.

8. *What is meant by the Immaculate Conception of Mary? by the virgin birth of Jesus?*

By the Immaculate Conception we mean "that the Blessed Virgin Mary, in the first instant of her conception, by a singular privilege and grace granted by God, in view of the merits of Jesus Christ, the Savior of the human race, was preserved exempt from all stain of original sin" [Pius IX, *Ineffabilis*]. Christ's merits can remove sin from the soul or prevent sin from getting into the soul. In our case, Christ's redemption cleanses the soul from original sin; in Mary's case, it prevented original sin from ever staining her soul.

By the virgin birth of Jesus, we mean that Jesus had no human father but was conceived and born miraculously through the supernatural operation of the Holy Ghost. Mary was a virgin, before, during, and after the conception and the birth of her Divine Son (cf. *The Catholic Encyclopedia*).

9. *Justify five of the titles given to Mary in the Litany of the Blessed Virgin Mary (or assign one or two different ones to each member of the class).*

1) *Holy Mother of God.* Christ was God. Mary was His Mother. Therefore she is the Mother of God.

2) *Mother of our Savior.* Christ is our Savior. She is His Mother. Therefore she is the Mother of our Savior.

3) *Refuge of Sinners.* All who pray to Mary are led by her to Jesus who forgives them their sins.

4) *Cause of Our Joy.* She alone is sinless. Yet she was entirely human just as we are. Therefore we rejoice at her great grace.

5) *Queen of all Saints.* She alone is sinless. Even original sin did not stain her soul. All other saints had at least the stain of original sin.

6) *Queen of Martyrs.* Mary is the Queen of Martyrs because she shared more deeply than any one else in the Martyrdom of her Divine Son.

7) *Vessel of Honor.* Mary became the most honored vessel — the vessel into which was poured God's greatest gift, namely, the Hypostatic Union.

24.

CHRIST AND THE APOSTLES

Problem Questions, Chap. XXV, p. 215.

1. *Name the twelve Apostles.*

Peter, Andrew, James, John, Phillip, Bartholomew, Matthew, and Thomas, James the son of Alpheus, Simon, Jude, and Judas Iscariot.

2. *Describe how Christ called them.*

Christ selected twelve special disciples whom He called Apostles (Luke vi. 13–16), (cf. page 204). Some of the Apostles were called individually: Peter, James, and John (Luke v. 10–11). Matthew's call is found in Matt. ix. 9; Mark ii. 14; Luke v. 27.

3. *Write the life of Peter.*

The Life of Peter (cf. *New Catholic Dictionary,* Art. "Peter"). Simon, son of Jona, was a fisherman of Bethsaida a town on Lake Genesareth. He was one of the disciples of John the Baptist. Jesus named him Peter and appointed him head of the apostolic band and the head of His Church. He was later the first bishop of Rome, and as bishop of Rome, pope of the universal Church. He died a martyr's death at Rome during the persecution of Nero (A.D. 64–68) by being crucified head downward.

4. *Describe Judas' betrayal of Christ. How was the Apostle chosen in place of Judas? What was his name?*

Betrayal of Judas (cf. page 210). Matthew's account: "As He yet spoke, behold Judas, one of the twelve, came, and with him a great multitude with swords and clubs, sent from the chief priests and the ancients of the people. And he that betrayed Him gave them a sign, saying: Whomsoever I shall kiss, that is He, hold Him fast. And forthwith coming to Jesus he said: Hail, Rabbi. And he kissed Him. And Jesus said to him: Friend, where to art thou come? Then they came up, and laid hands on Jesus, and held Him" (Matt. xxvi. 47–50).

Matthias was chosen in place of Judas: "And they appointed two, Joseph called Barsabas, who was surnamed Justus, and Matthias. And praying, they said Thou, Lord, who knowest the hearts of all, show whether of these two Thou hast chosen, to take the place of this ministry and apostleship, from which Judas hath by transgression fallen, that he might go to his own place. And they gave them lots, and the lot fell upon Matthias, and he was numbered with the eleven Apostles" (Acts i. 23–26).

5. Describe the Apostles in general. Were they an exceptional group of men in any way? Why do you think Christ selected such a group?

The Apostles were men chosen from the ordinary walks of life, fishermen, tax collectors, etc. Christ chose such men because unlike the proud and learned Pharisees they were more humble and were willing to learn our Lord's doctrine. God frequently chooses lowly and humble men as instruments of His designs in order to show that the works which they accomplished are due not to human endeavors but solely to the grace of God. As St. Paul says: "But the foolish things of the world hath God chosen, that He may confound the wise; and the weak things of the world hath God chosen, that He may confound the strong. And the base things of the world, and the things that are contemptible, hath God chosen, and things that are not, that He might bring to nought things that are: That no flesh should glory in His sight" (I Cor. i. 27–29).

6. Keeping in mind yourself and other human beings that you know well, what do you think of the denials of Christ, the betrayal of Christ, and the misunderstandings of Christ's kingdom among the Apostles?

Cf. Chapter XXVI, question 5, p. 114.

7. *Describe the conversion of Paul.*

Conversion of Paul. Cf. Acts ix. 1–22. Also page 212 of text.

8. *Write the life of Paul.*

Life of Paul, the Apostle of the Gentiles (Cf. *New Catholic Dictionary,* Art. "Paul"). He was born at Tarsus in Cilicia about A.D. 2, and martyred in Rome about A.D. 66. He was a Jew of the tribe of Benjamin and received the name Saul. He was educated at the school of Gamaliel in Jerusalem (Acts xxii. 3). He persecuted the Christians and witnessed the martyrdom of St. Stephen. His conversion occurred miraculously while he was journeying to Damascus where he had intended to seize the Christians. After this he became a most zealous follower of Christ and by his missionary work in far countries earned for himself the name "Apostle of the Gentiles." He made three long journeys into foreign lands and it was on the first of these that he became known as Paul.

9. *Draw a map of the missionary journeys of Paul.*

For a map of St. Paul's journeys, see Map 15 of the Holy Bible, Rheims-Douay version. A short account of St. Paul's three journeys: all have a common starting point, namely, Antioch. On the first journey he visited the island of Cyprus and southwestern Asia Minor. On the second, he visited Lystra, Philippi, Thessalonica, Athens, Corinth, Ephesus, and returned to Jerusalem. On the third journey he followed almost the exact course of the second and the most notable stopping places were Philippi, Athens, Corinth, and Ephesus.

10. *Make a collection of pictures in which the Apostles are portrayed. List them, give name of author, and write a sentence telling what you think is the most striking thing in the picture.*

Consult the Bible History and holy pictures in which the Apostles are portrayed.

25.

THE HOLY GHOST ON PENTECOST

Problem Questions, Chap. XXVI, p. 224.

1. *What promises were made in advance that the Holy Ghost would come?*

Scriptural texts containing the promise of the Holy Ghost: John xv. 26; xiv. 26; xvi. 7; xiv. 16; xiv. 23; xiv. 17. From the Old Testament: "And it shall come to pass after this, that I will pour out My spirit upon all flesh; and your sons and your daughters shall prophesy: your old men shall dream dreams, and your young men shall see visions. Moreover upon My servants and handmaids in those days I will pour forth My spirit" (Joel ii. 28–29).

2. *Describe the descent of the Holy Ghost on the Apostles.*

On Pentecost, fifty days after the Resurrection and ten days after the Ascension of our Lord into heaven, the Holy Ghost, the third Person of the Blessed Trinity, descended upon the Apostles in the form of tongues of fire (cf. page 219).

3. *Select the picture of the Descent of the Holy Ghost on the Apostles which you like best, and tell why.*

Pictures of the Descent of the Holy Ghost on the Apostles: Giotto, Gaddi, Titian, Fra Angelico, Donatello (cf. *The Gospel Story in Art*, by John La Farge).

4. *What happened to the Apostles as a result of the descent of the Holy Ghost?*

The gift of tongues: The Apostles spoke the mother tongue of all the different nations enumerated in Acts ii. 9–11. In these tongues — hitherto unknown to them — they spoke the wonderful works of God. Each one in the audience was naturally drawn to listen to the Apostle who was speaking in his own language.

"We have heard them speak in our own tongues the wonderful works of God" (Acts ii. 11).

The Apostles were made strong in their faith and they boldly taught the doctrines of Christ. Doubt, ignorance, and misgivings were replaced by faith, knowledge, and understanding.

5. *Go back now and read your answers to the question (Chap. XXV) keeping in mind yourself and other human beings you know well, what do you think of the denials of Christ, the betrayal of Christ, and the misunderstandings of Christ's kingdom among the Apostles?*

St. Peter was inclined to presumption; Judas to covetousness. Neither resisted his principal weakness in its first beginnings and in its first manifestations. Venial sins frequently lead to serious falls and sins. Christ permitted the fall of Peter and the betrayal of Judas in order to show to the world that the stability of His Church would not be destroyed by the scandals which would come.

The Apostles did not understand at first that Christ's kingdom would be purely spiritual. They thought His kingdom would be material and temporal in which each one could advance his own ambitions.

26.

THE ROMAN CATHOLIC CHURCH

Problem Questions, Chap. XXVII, pp. 237, 238.

1. *What was the purpose of Christ, the Son of God, in becoming man?*

Christ came upon earth to restore to us — though not in the same form — the gifts which we lost in the fall of Adam. Christ, who was God-man, repaired the offenses done to God by our sins, merited sanctifying grace for us, and opened to us the gates of heaven. He merited sufficient actual graces for us to overcome our evil tendencies. He also conquered death by meriting for us our future resurrection of the body. As teacher He taught us the truths of salvation and pointed out to us the way to heaven.

2. How does the fulfillment of such a purpose require the establishment of an institution to carry on the work of the Redemption?

Since Christ did not wish to remain visibly in human society until the end of the world, He established an institution which would transmit His teachings infallibly and in their entirety. This institution was also to govern His flock and through its priesthood and sacraments dispense His graces.

3. What is the name of the institution which Christ established to continue, or through which He might act after the Ascension?

The Roman Catholic Church.

4. When was the Roman Catholic Church established?

The *St. Andrew's Daily Missal* in its explanatory notes says that Pentecost is "the birth of the Church" (p. 952). "Jesus laid the foundation of the Church during His Apostolic life, and conferred on her His powers after the Resurrection. It was left for the Holy Ghost to complete the training of the Apostles and to endow them with Divine strength" (p. 964).

5. What promise was made to the Church regarding the Holy Ghost? regarding Christ Himself?

Christ promised that He would ask the Father to send the Holy Ghost who would abide with the Church forever (cf. pp. 225–226). Christ said that He would be with the Church all days even to the consummation of the world (Matt. xxviii. 19–20).

6. What is meant by Paraclete?

Paraclete (Greek, advocate or consoler), is an appellation of the Holy Ghost. Christ promised to send the Apostles "another Paraclete" (John xiv. 16), so that they might not be desolate when He departs. Christ was the first advocate or comforter and He continues His advocacy for us in heaven (John xi. 1). The

Holy Ghost, the Paraclete, is the advocate in the Church, who pleads God's cause with men, who keeps the Church from error, and sanctifies souls through the ministry of the word and of the Sacraments (*Catholic Dictionary*, Art. "Paraclete").

7. What is the relation of the Church to Christ? If it were possible to conceive it, what meaning would the Church have without Christ?

Christ says, "I am the vine and you are the branches." St. Paul affirms that Christ is the head of the Church and the faithful are the body. The Church, then, is the Mystic Body of Christ, and since Christ, the source of all grace, is the head of that Body, it is through Him that all the members of the Body receive grace. A Church without Christ would be like a body without a head.

8. What do you mean by the statement that the Church is the Body of Christ?

See answer to the preceding question.

9. Why must the Church of Christ be One? Holy? Catholic? Apostolic?

The Church must be One, Holy, Catholic, and Apostolic (cf. pp. 228–229).

10. What church has these four marks of the true Church of Christ?

The Catholic Church alone has these four marks.

11. What is meant by the words "indefectibility," "authority," "infallibility"?

Indefectibility — not liable to defect, failure, or decay.

Authority — legal or rightful power; a right to command or act.

Infallibility — quality or state of being infallible; not capable of erring, failing, or deceiving.

12. In what ways are the attributes of the Church, indefectibility, authority, and infallibility, directly traceable to Christ?

These three attributes are directly traceable to Christ (cf. *Highway to God*, pp. 230–231).

13. Through what instruments does the infallibility of the Church of Christ express itself?

The infallibility of the Church expresses itself through general councils and through the pope.

14. What is a general council of the Church? How many have been held?

A general council is a legally convened assembly of ecclesiastical dignitaries and theological experts representing the entire Church for the purpose of discussing, defining, and regulating matters of Church doctrine and discipline. The members of the council cannot act independently of the supreme pontiff, who presides over the assembly in person or by delegate; and no decree has binding force until it is confirmed by him. (*Cath. Ency.*) Twenty general councils have been held. See *Highway to God*, p. 231.

15. What is meant by the body of the Church?

To belong to the body of the Church means to be an actual member of that actual visible society, the Roman Catholic Church, that is, to be one of the number of those who profess the same faith in Jesus Christ, participate in the same sacraments, and are subject to the same lawful pastors, the bishops, under one visible head, the pope, the bishop of Rome.

16. What is meant by the soul of the Church?

The phrase the "body" and the "soul" of the Church is variously used. In Gasparri's *The Catholic Catechism*, p. 99, the "body" and the "soul" of the Church are defined as follows:
"(134) *What is meant by the 'body of the Church'?*"

By the 'body of the Church' is meant what is visible in the

Church and makes the Church herself visible — namely, the faithful themselves in so far as they are one body, also external forms of government, external authority, outward profession of faith, the administration of the Sacraments, ritual worship, etc.

(135) *What is meant by the 'soul of the Church'?*

By the 'soul of the Church' is meant the invisible principle of the spiritual and supernatural life of the Church — namely, the ever-present assistance of the Holy Ghost, the principle of authority, inward obedience to rule, habitual grace, and the infused virtues, etc. [140]" [1]

This, however, is not the meaning in which the words are used in this and the preceding question. In our questions it applies to the members of the Church and a fuller significance of the questions may be found in Gasparri's *Catholic Catechism*, pp. 106–108, questions and answers 157–164, especially 157, 162, 163, 165.

As the phrase "the soul of the Church" has been used in connection with the *Baltimore Catechism* it includes the following type of persons, who are not being members of the actual visible society which is the Roman Catholic Church:

"(162) *Can an adult person who dies unbaptized be saved?*

An adult person who dies unbaptized can be saved not only

    i. if he has faith at least as regards those truths which must of necessity be believed, since they are the necessary means of salvation, and that charity which supplies the place of Baptism; but also

    ii. if, through the operation of God's light and grace, he is — despite his invincible ignorance of the true religion — prepared to obey God and has been careful to keep the natural law.[160]

(163) *Can an adult person who has been validly baptized but, through no fault of his own, belongs to a heretical or schismatical body be saved?*

An adult person who has been validly baptized but through no fault of his own belongs to a heretical or schismatic body can be saved, provided he has not lost the grace received in Baptism, or if, after losing it by sin, he regains it by due repentance.[161]

---

[1]The Catholic Catechism, drawn up by His Eminence Peter Cardinal Gasparri, p. 99. P. J. Kenedy and Sons, New York, 482 pp.

(165) *What are those bound to do who are outside the Church, but are in doubt about their state?*

Those who are outside the Church but are in doubt about their state are in duty bound sincerely to seek the truth 'in the Lord,' to learn as far as they can Christ's teaching set before them, and — when they have recognized which is the true Church of Christ — to enter her."[2]

The material here presented furnishes some of the basic material for an explanation of the statement: "There is no salvation outside the Church." Cf. also the full statement in Gasparri's Appendix vi. pp. 307–310.

17. *Who are members of the soul but not of the body of the Church?*

Those outside of the Catholic Church, not being members of Christ's Mystical Body, do not belong to the soul of the Church, even though they are in good faith. They can, however, have the Holy Spirit and thus belong to Him who is the soul of the Church. (Cf. "The Church" — Papers from the Summer School of Catholic Studies held at Cambridge, pp. 85–86.)

18. *What is meant by the Church Militant, the Church Suffering, and the Church Triumphant?*

The Church Militant embraces all the living members of the Catholic Church. The Church Suffering embraces all the suffering souls in purgatory. The Church Triumphant embraces all those who have satisfied for their sins and are now in heaven.

19. *Of what part of the Church are you a member? Of what part is St. Francis of Assisi? Of what part are the souls in purgatory?*

We are now members of the Church Militant, because we are still living. St. Francis of Assisi is a member of the Church Triumphant in heaven. The souls in purgatory are members of the Church Suffering.

---

[2]*Ibid.*, pp. 107–108.

20. *What is meant by the Communion of Saints? What does saints in this connection mean? Are you a saint?*

Communion of Saints (cf. Text, pp. 234–235). It includes all who belong to the Church Militant, Suffering, and Triumphant. The word "saint" is used here as a general name for Christian.

27.

GRACE AND THE SACRAMENTS

Problem Questions, Chap. XXVIII, pp. 252, 253.

1. What is grace? Why is it called the "life of the soul"?

Grace is a supernatural gift granted to man by God to help him attain eternal life. Grace is called the "life of the soul" because it is the vivifying principle which brings the soul back to supernatural life when it is spiritually dead in mortal sin. Grace, which is superadded to a soul already possessing grace, raises it to a higher participation in the divine life. The Blessed Trinity, the Source of all life, dwells in the soul which is in the state of grace. Finally our life as active members of the Mystical Body of Christ is possible only through grace which flows from Christ, the Head, to the members, uniting them in one living organism.

2. What relation is there between the doctrine of grace and Adam?

There is a direct and important relation between the doctrine of grace and Adam. When Adam was created, God raised him to a supernatural state by giving him sanctifying grace. This was necessary if Adam were one day to merit heaven. But, by the Fall Adam lost this grace and fell from the supernatural state. In this fallen condition Adam could not hope ever to attain eternal life with God. However, God in His love for man, sent His only Son to make amends for sin and win back the things lost by Adam when he fell. By His life, suffering, death, and resurrection, Christ regained for all mankind grace which is so necessary for this eternal life with God.

121

3. Who is the single source of grace?

God is the single source of grace because grace is essentially a participation in the divine life. God alone can grant, and be the source of this gift.

4. What is the meaning of "sacrament"?

"Sacrament" means an outward or sensible sign which indicates and gives inward or invisible grace. It is an efficacious symbol which, because Christ has chosen it for that purpose, produces grace in the soul.

5. What are the three necessary marks of a sacrament?

The three marks or inherent characteristics necessary for a sacrament are the following:

1) It must be a sign discernible by the senses.
2) It must have been instituted by Christ.
3) It must give grace.

6. Make a list of the "outward signs" of each sacrament.

Signs of each sacrament:

1) Baptism — water and the words, "I baptize thee in the Name of the Father and of the Son and of the Holy Ghost" (cf. Chap. 29).

2) Confirmation — holy chrism and the anointing and words by the bishop (cf. Chap. 36).

3) Holy Eucharist — bread and wine and the words of consecration in the Mass (cf. Chap. 33).

4) Penance — confession of sins, act of contrition, satisfaction for sins, and the absolution of the priest (cf. Chaps. 30–31).

5) Extreme Unction — the anointing of the five senses with the oil of the sick, and the words of the priest (cf. Chap. 38).

6) Holy Orders — the imposition of the hands by the bishop and the handing to the candidate the instruments of his office, at the same time pronouncing the words prescribed by the Pontifical (cf. Chap. 39).

7) Matrimony — the two persons and their words of mutual consent "I do" (cf. Chap. 37).

7. *Discuss the sacraments as channels of grace.*

The sacraments are called the channels of grace because God has ordained that through them graces merited for us by Christ shall be distributed to all men who are properly disposed to receive them. To use an analogy: we may compare grace which is the sustaining principle of our spiritual life to food and air which maintain our physical life. Food is taken into the stomach and air into the lungs whence these two substances are transmitted by the blood stream into the human organism where it is utilized for processes of living, growing, repairing, etc. So the sacraments like the blood stream transmit graces to the various members of that Mystical Body for the purpose of giving them spiritual life and growth in holiness and of repairing the damages of sin. To extend the analogy still farther we may note that just as the blood carrying these life-giving substances takes various routes and passes through various kinds of arteries, veins, and capillaries so also in the distribution of grace there are seven distinct sacraments each having its own proper function.

8. *Do the outward signs of each sacrament actually give the grace, or are they only outward signs or symbols of it?*

The outward signs of each sacrament actually give the grace of themselves. They are not just symbols of this grace. Thus these signs are called "efficacious symbols" meaning symbols which effect or cause grace by virtue of the power placed in them by Christ when He instituted them.

9. *What is sanctifying grace?*

Sanctifying grace is a supernatural gift of God by which we are made holy and pleasing to God. By this grace the Holy Trinity dwells in the soul and the person receiving it partakes of the divine life which raises him to a perfection necessary to attain heaven. This grace is a permanent quality which remains in the soul as long as no mortal sin is committed.

10. *What is actual grace?*

Actual grace is a supernatural and transient help by which God illumines the intellect and aids the will in the performance of supernatural acts.

11. *If by sacramental grace we mean the special grace which each sacrament gives, show that sacramental graces are actual graces.*

Sacramental graces are actual graces because they give us the assistance necessary to perform the supernatural acts which are the goal of each sacrament. Actual graces are a help to perform good actions. Thus, baptism gives a sacramental grace which enables us to live good Christian lives befitting adopted sons of God. Penance helps us to resist temptations. Confirmation helps us to be brave and strong in the service of God and His Church. And so on through each of the sacraments which give a special grace to do the things God requires of us.

12. *If the sacraments gave only one grace, show that there would be need but for a single sacrament.*

If the sacraments gave only one grace, then the grace given by each of the sacraments would be identically the same. Hence there would be need but for one sacrament since this would be just as efficacious as seven. But we know that Christ instituted seven sacraments so it remains that each sacrament has a special function which it alone performs. There is need for exactly seven sacraments in order that all of man's needs be cared for in the sacramental system.

13. *Who is the sole source of the power of the sacraments?*

Christ is the sole source of the power of the sacraments because they were instituted by His divine power; and the merits distributed by the sacraments were gained for man by our Lord's life, passion, and death.

14. *Does each sacrament give sanctifying grace?*

All the sacraments give sanctifying grace if the recipient places no obstacle in the way, that is, if they are received worthily and with the proper intention.

15. *What is meant by the divine virtues of Faith, Hope, and Charity? Are these also natural virtues?*

The divine virtues of Faith, Hope, and Charity are dispositions of the soul. They come into the soul together with sanctifying grace. Faith helps us to believe firmly in the truths of our religion, especially those which cannot be entirely understood. Hope is that disposition of the soul by which we have confidence that God will aid us in our efforts to save our souls and be happy with Him in heaven. Charity is that gift which helps us to love God with our whole heart and soul, and our neighbor as ourself. These virtues, as explained above, are supernatural virtues because they help us to do things pertaining to God and to the Beatific Vision in heaven. There are also the natural virtues of faith, hope, and charity which we use in our daily lives. For example: we may have faith that a check for one hundred dollars really represents that much money; we may hope for a fair day, or we may love our parents.

16. *What is the difference between the sacraments of the living and the sacraments of the dead?*

Grace is the life of the soul, and sin is the cause of spiritual death. Those who have original or mortal sin on their souls receive the sacraments of the dead, baptism and penance. These two give grace to the soul and make it live. The other sacraments are received by those who are already in the state of grace. They add grace to the soul which is living and are called sacraments of the living. Hence we see that the first give life by taking away death, the others raise the soul up to a higher perfection of life.

17. *Show the usefulness of having only the sacraments of baptism, confirmation, and holy orders leave a mark (charisma) on the soul.*

The sacraments of baptism, confirmation, and holy orders impress an indelible character on the soul marking the person perpetually as a Christian, a soldier, and a priest, respectively. This mark designates the special dignity or status of the person who bears it eternally. Nothing, not even sin, effaces this character inhering in these three sacraments and it remains forever unchanged, to the glory of those who are saved and to the shame of those who are lost.

It is becoming and useful that these three sacraments should impress a mark on the soul. For whoever is deputed for some special function and receives power to this end, should be designated by some mark in order to be distinguishable from the rest. Now, by these three sacraments the faithful are empowered to perform special functions. By baptism a man becomes a member and a citizen of the Church, and receives the passive power of receiving the other sacraments. By confirmation he becomes a soldier of Christ and receives the power of doing those things which pertain to spiritual warfare. By holy orders he becomes a minister of Christ and a leader of His army, and receives the active power of administering the other sacraments.

18. *What is the effect of the unworthy reception of the sacraments?*

If a sacrament is unworthily received it fails to give the grace which is attached to it, and the recipient commits a sacrilege.

19. *What are sacramentals? How do they operate? Name five sacramentals.*

Sacramentals are certain visible signs, objects, or ceremonials instituted by the Church to help the faithful dispose themselves for the reception of grace. They are material representations of spiritual realities, making it easier for us to direct our mind to supernatural objects. They do not give grace of themselves as the sacraments do; but, by their use, we are brought closer to the means of grace. Indulgences are often attached to the use of sacramentals. Some of the sacramentals are: rosary beads, statues, holy water, stations of the cross, the sign of the cross.

28.

BAPTISM

Problem Questions, Chap. XXIX, pp. 260–261.

1. *Baptism is an initiation ceremony. Into what society does baptism admit one? May one, after joining, leave it at will?*

Baptism makes us members of the Church of Christ. Such a membership is perpetual because of the indelible character which baptism imprints upon the soul. Hence a baptized person cannot leave the Church at will but always remains a member.

2. *Before going "over the top," Shocky Roder, who had been given that nickname on account of a heavy head of hair, said to his Catholic friend: "Jerry, I have never been baptized; I want to be a Catholic. Won't you baptize me since there is no priest around?" Jerry, a devout Catholic, eager for the opportunity, obtained some fresh water, poured it directly over the top of Shocky's head, saying at the same time, "I baptize thee in the name of the Father, and of the Son, and of the Holy Ghost." Did Shocky receive the sacrament of baptism? Explain. If not actually, was Shocky's desire for baptism enough should he have been killed? Discuss.*

The water must flow over the skin for the valid reception of the sacrament of baptism. Jerry, who poured water directly over the top of Shocky's head, saying at the same time: "I baptize thee in the name of the Father, and of the Son, and of the Holy Ghost," doubtfully conferred the sacrament. If Shocky's heavy head of hair prevented the flow of water over the skin, the sacrament was invalid. If, however, the water did flow over the skin, the baptism was valid. Either of the two possibilities is probable, hence the sacrament was doubtfully received. In order to remove this doubt, conditional baptism must be given. The conditional administration is not a second baptism because this sacrament can be received only once. It has its effect on the soul only when the previous doutbful baptism was invalid.

Shocky's desire for baptism was not enough alone, should he have been killed. Baptism of desire demands a perfect act of contrition or a perfect love of God together with the explicit or implicit (implied, though not expressed) desire of receiving the sacrament.

3. *The story is told of a certain man who on the day after his confirmation learned that he had been baptized with milk. Why was the man's baptism not valid? What would have to be done in a case of this kind?*

True and natural water is the only valid matter for the sacrament of baptism. The man in the story, who on the day after confirmation, learned that he had been baptized with milk, was in reality not baptized. Milk is not true and natural water. Since he was not baptized previous to his reception of confirmation, that sacrament was likewise invalid. The sacrament of baptism, which is the door to all the others, is necessary for the valid reception of the other six sacraments. It would be necessary for him to be baptized and only afterwards to receive confirmation.

4. *A man, alone in the woods, accidentally shot himself. He had never been baptized but had often thought of taking the final step and had learned the essentials of baptism. Knowing that he would never be able to leave the woods alive, he succeeded in getting his canteen open and with the words: "I baptize thee in the name of the Father, and of the Son, and of the Holy Ghost," poured water over his head. Was the man baptized? Discuss.*

In the sacrament of baptism there is required a distinct subject and a distinct minister. This cannot be dispensed with even in the case of grave necessity. The man, because he acted both as subject and minister, did not receive the sacrament.

5. *In a certain grade school which a few Protestant children attended, the teacher had been explaining the sacrament of baptism. At the noon recess, two of the girls had succeeded, as they said, "in baptizing" one of their Protestant friends in spite of violent protests. Had they succeeded? Discuss.*

The intention of receiving baptism as a sacred thing is required for the valid reception of the sacrament. The two Catholic girls, who attempted to baptize their Protestant friend in spite of violent protest, failed to do so. When baptism is administered against a person's will it is invalid and thus it is without effect.

6. *Mr. Solberg, a baptized Lutheran, joined the Catholic Church and received conditional baptism. Why did Mr. Solberg receive conditional baptism? Are his sins forgiven by this conditional baptism? Explain.*

Mr. Solberg, a baptized Lutheran, was now baptized conditionally because there was a doubt as to the validity of his previous baptism. The Church does this to make sure that the person is really baptized. It is not a second baptism because this sacrament can be received only once. The conditional administration is without effect if the person has validly received the sacrament previously. The true state of the soul is unknown so the Church insists also on confession with conditional absolution. Thus it is that either the conditional baptism or the conditional absolution has its effect on the soul — never both. If the previous baptism was valid, then the sacrament of penance takes away all actual sins; if the conditional baptism is valid, then it takes away original sin as well as all actual sin.

7. *Mrs. Kelly, whose father is a devout Catholic but whose mother is a Protestant, earnestly desires her parents to be sponsors for her infant daughter in baptism. May Mrs. Kelly's parents be sponsors? Discuss.*

Mrs. Kelly's mother, who is a non-Catholic, may not be a sponsor for her daughter's child. It is most probable that, if the parents die or fail in their duty, a Protestant would not attend to the proper spiritual and religious training of the child. The Church, which has learned from centuries of experience, requires certain things of a person who is to become a sponsor. Thus it is that she will not allow a Protestant this privilege which carries with it such a sacred duty.

Mrs. Kelly's father, who is a devout Catholic, may act as an only sponsor for his daughter's child; Canon Law says that — strictly speaking — one sponsor will suffice.

8. *John, a fourteen-year-old boy and a close friend of the Ross family, had been asked to be sponsor in baptism for Mary Anne. After a period of twenty years, a friendship so close had grown up between John and Mary Anne that they wished to marry. What must John and Mary Anne do? Why?*

A person baptized contracts a spiritual relationship with the sponsor. Such a relationship constitutes a diriment impediment, making it impossible for the two parties to validly marry. For a very good reason, however, the bishop may see fit to dispense from the impediment.

29.

THE CONFESSION OF SINS

Problem Questions, Chap. XXXI, pp. 279, 280.

1. *Mrs. Seidel admits the necessity of everyone to have a trustworthy friend yet she says, "Confession is an invention of priests." From a purely human point of view, how can we argue the value of the confessional? What has been your personal reaction in this respect?*

Even from the human point of view, the confessional has a great value. Sin is the greatest trouble man has, and if one admits the need of a trustworthy friend to whom other troubles may be confided, he surely ought to see the value of the confessional. Nothing is so disquieting to man as remorse of conscience, as a conscience that bothers him and reproaches him with his sins.

In confession man is restored to peace and happiness. In confession man unburdens his troubles and exposes the inmost thoughts of his soul — under safeguards which are far more secure and better than those afforded by a psycho-analyst or even a trustworthy friend. Many a person who has come to a correct understanding of this sacrament has found in it a regular and certain source of contentment, peace, and joy (cf. page 274 of Text).

2. Ned Black was caught in the act of stealing a large sum of money. He was arrested and sentenced. Ned was sorry he stole the money because he was caught. Ned has contrition. Is this contrition enough for the reception of the sacrament of penance? Why? How must contrition be? Why must contrition precede the confession of sins?

No, Ned's contrition is not sufficient for the sacrament of penance, because it is based solely on natural motives. Contrition must be supernatural, that is, our sorrow must be prompted by the grace of God and brought about by motives which spring from faith — and not merely because of what will happen to us on earth or because of similar purely natural motives.

Contrition must precede the confession of sins, because the sins cannot be forgiven unless we are sorry for them.

3. One penitent accuses himself by saying, "I missed Sunday Mass five or ten times"; another, "I sinned against the First Commandment, the Second Commandment, the Fourth Commandment," etc.; a third, "I sinned in thought, word, and deed"; a fourth, "I stole"; and a fifth, "I spoke improper words." What is wrong with all these statements? How must one's confession be made? How might each one of these statements be made in the right way so as to eliminate the necessity of the priest's asking questions?

These statements all fail to give either the exact nature of the sin or the exact number of times the sin was committed. One's confession should be *entire*, that is, including the number and kinds of sins and the circumstances which change their nature.

Corrected statements:

1) "I missed Sunday Mass . . . . (exact number or as near as possible) times when I could have gone."

2) "I sinned against the First Commandment (Second or Third) by . . . . (tell what wrong has been done), ... (number of times)."

3) "I sinned in thought by thinking of . . . . (tell what) . . . . (number of times). I sinned in word by saying . . . . (tell what) . . . . (number of times). I sinned in deed by doing . . . . (tell what) . . . . (number of times)."

4) "I stole . . . . (tell what was stolen) . . . . (number of times)."

5) "I spoke improper words about . . . . (what) . . . . (number of times)."

4. *Francis McDougall has been a daily communicant for some time and now very rarely falls into serious sin. He goes to confession weekly and has again and again been requested by his confessor to include a sin from his past life. Why does the confessor request this? What is a good way to end all confessions?*

Absolution means taking away sin. If the penitent has not confessed any real sin, the sacred words of the absolution would be pronounced by the priest to no purpose. A person has to be sorry for and confess at least one actual sin in order to receive validly the sacrament of penance. The confessor asks this question of Francis, who has been leading a good life, in order to make sure that his confession includes at least one actual sin, either venial or mortal, and not merely slight imperfections which if confessed by themselves would not be enough for the priest to give absolution. A good way to end every confession is to say, "I also accuse myself of all the sins of my past life, especially . . . (mentioning a particular sin of your past life)."

5. *Discuss the words of St. Augustine: "Accuse thyself, and God will excuse thee; excuse thyself and God will accuse thee."*

St. Augustine's pithy sentence is another way of saying, "If you admit that you were at fault and are really sorry for having sinned, God will forgive you. But if, on the other hand, you are stubborn and will not admit your wrongs nor be sorry for them, God cannot forgive your sins and will accuse you of them on the Judgment Day."

30.

THE SACRAMENT OF THE HOLY EUCHARIST

Problem Questions, Chap. XXXIII, pp. 295, 296.

1. *Protestant religions in general teach that our Lord is present in the Holy Eucharist only spiritually, and is only spiritually received, and that the words of our Lord, "This is My Body," are to be understood as meaning, "This is a symbol of My Body; partake in memory of Me." What is the correct meaning of our Lord's words? What is the Sacrament of the Eucharist? How do we know that Christ is present in this sacrament?*

The correct meaning of our Lord's words is exactly what the words themselves imply. When He took the bread in His hands and said, "This is My Body," our Lord meant "This which still looks, tastes, and feels like bread is not bread any more but is now really and truly My Body." When He said, "This is My Blood," He again meant just what He said; the wine, without changing in appearance, has ceased to be wine and through the power of God has become the true Blood of our Lord. When Christ said, "Do this in commemoration of Me," He was giving to the Apostles and the priests of the future the power to do what He had just done, "Do *this*," He said, in other words, "change bread and wine into My true Body and Blood." Had our Lord — without giving any explanation — attributed some new and unusual meaning to these simple words, He would have deceived the people.

The Sacrament of the Eucharist is the Sacrament which contains the Body and Blood, Soul and Divinity, of our Lord Jesus Christ, under the appearances of bread and wine.

We know that Christ is present in this Sacrament because the Catholic Church, the infallible teacher and interpreter of Scripture, tells us so.

2. *Steve Ross, one day talking about the Real Presence with an intimate Catholic friend, Jim Nevon, put the question: "If you believe that Christ is really present in that tiny wafer, tell me how He got there." Answer for Jim. Name the principal parts of the Mass. What is the best way to take part in the Mass? Why?*

Jim should answer that Christ becomes present in the white particle during Mass at the part called the Consecration. The priest pronounces over the bread the same words used by Christ at the Last Supper, and at that moment — because of the power given by Christ to His priests — the white particle ceases to be bread and becomes Christ's Body, just as happened at the Last Supper.

The Mass is made up of two essential parts: the introductory part comprises the Preparation and Instruction, and is known as the Mass of the Catechumens; the second part comprises the Offertory, Consecration, Communion, and Thanksgiving, and is known as the Mass of the Faithful (cf. page 311 of Text).

The best way to take part in the Mass is to offer the Mass to God with the priest (by saying the same or similar prayers from a Missal or prayer book) and to receive Holy Communion. By doing so we actively participate in the Sacrifice of Christ, the most perfect act of religion, which has more value than all our other prayers and good works combined; by receiving Holy Communion every time we assist at Mass, we participate more fully in the Mass and make the Sacrifice of the Mass more intimately our own — at the same time nourishing and strengthening our souls by the reception of the Heavenly Food so necessary for the life of the soul.

3. Jack Ertman forgot to mention a serious sin in confession. He thought of it immediately after he had left the confessional. He is a Knight of Columbus and very much desires to receive Holy Communion on the morrow with the other members of the organization. Is Jack in the state of grace? Discuss. If without great inconvenience he could go back to the confessional should he do so? Explain.

Yes, Jack is in the state of grace. Although he forgot to mention the serious sin in confession, it was indirectly forgiven. A person is bound to confess all his unforgiven mortal sins which can be recalled after a reasonable examination of conscience. If he should forget a sin and therefore unintentionally omit it from his confession, that sin would be forgiven along with the others; both the guilt and eternal punishment due to it would be taken away, and the forgiven person restored to the state of grace. Our Lord, who knows our failings better than anyone else, instituted confession to help us, not to become a terrible burden. One's confession cannot, therefore, be unworthy because of some reason for which he is not responsible — such as poor memory. However, indirect forgiveness of sin is only an extraordinary means given by God to assist the penitent who without blame omits a sin from his confession. If the sin is later remembered, it must be confessed. It is not necessary to go again to confession immediately, but the sin must be told the next time the person goes to confession. If he should again forget it, he would have to tell it at the next confession at which it was remembered. The reason for this is that the sacrament of penance is the ordinary means given by our Lord for the forgiveness of sins; all serious sins committed after baptism are to be confessed in that sacrament for the purpose of obtaining forgiveness.

If Jack could without great inconvenience go back to confession, he should do so. This may be advisable for the greater peace of his soul. It would also avoid his forgetting the sin at his next confession.

4. *About two weeks ago a certain engineer had the misfortune of falling into serious sin. On a Sunday morning he got into the city just in time to attend an eight o'clock Mass. At Communion time of the Mass he very much desired to receive yet hesitated because of the consciousness of serious sin. Upon second thought, he made an act of perfect contrition and approached the Holy Table. Was he in the state of grace? Discuss. Why may he not receive Holy Communion? Is he guilty of sin? Explain.*

If the engineer really made an act of perfect contrition, he was in the state of grace and received Holy Communion worthily. However, perfect contrition means sorrow for one's sins solely because they displease God who is Infinite Goodness. Since this kind of contrition may be rather difficult for some, our Lord has left us a means by which everyone can have his sins taken away with certainty, even though he has only imperfect contrition. This means instituted by our Lord is the sacrament of penance; and the Church rightly demands that anyone conscious of mortal sin, no matter how contrite he thinks himself, must go to confession before approaching the Holy Table.

If the engineer did not know of this requirement, he, of course, is not guilty of sin. One who is in good faith and not aware of doing something wrong, cannot commit sin by his act. However, when the engineer discovers the truth regarding this matter, he should, at the earliest opportunity, confess in the sacrament of penance the serious sin in question, even though it may already have been forgiven by the engineer's act of contrition. Only after such a confession has been made may he receive Holy Communion lawfully.

5. *Mrs. Thein has a very annoying cough. On Saturday she made a good confession with the intention of receiving Holy Communion the next day. Sunday morning her cough was particularly annoying, so she took a dose of cough medicine. May she receive Holy Communion? Discuss. Under what condition may one receive Holy Communion when not fasting?*

Mrs. Thein may not receive Holy Communion in this case, since she has broken the Eucharistic fast. The fast from midnight necessary for the reception of Holy Communion, includes abstinence from all things taken as food or drink, including medicine, even in small quantities. So the dose of cough medicine would prevent Mrs. Thein from receiving Holy Communion in this case.

Anyone who is in danger of death may receive Holy Communion even though he is not fasting.

6. *Miriam Steele understands as far as is possible to the human mind, the greatness of the Holy Eucharist; for this reason she feels unworthy to approach the Holy Table and remains away. Why is Miriam wrong? What words of Holy Scripture impress upon us the necessity of receiving the Body and Blood of Christ often? Why does the Church oblige the faithful to receive Holy Communion, at least once a year, during the Easter season?*

Miriam does not have the proper attitude toward the Holy Eucharist, because our Lord knew our unworthiness and yet He commanded that we receive His Body and Blood often and indicated that the more often we do so, the closer we shall come to Him. One can receive Holy Communion worthily, without being worthy of such an honor, for there can never be any equality between our worthiness and the Sacrament of the Eucharist. Christ left this Holy Sacrament not because we are already worthy but *to help make us worthy.*

The following words of Scripture impress upon us the necessity of receiving the Body and Blood of Christ often:

"Amen, amen I say unto you: Except you eat the Flesh of the Son of Man, and drink His Blood, you shall not have life in you."

"He that eateth My Flesh, and drinketh My Blood, hath everlasting life; and I will raise him up in the last day."

"For My Flesh is meat indeed; and My Blood is drink indeed."

"He that eateth My Flesh, and drinketh My Blood, abideth in Me, and I in him."

"As the living Father hath sent Me, and I live by the Father; so he that eateth Me, the same also shall live by Me."

"This is the Bread that came down from heaven. Not as your fathers did eat manna, and are dead. He that eateth this Bread, shall live forever" (John vi. 54–59).

The Church obliges the faithful to receive Holy Communion

at least once a year because she is solicitous for the welfare of the souls of her children. Holy Communion, being the Life of the soul and the most effective means for overcoming temptation and avoiding sin, cannot be neglected for more than a year without grievous harm to the soul.

7. *Dick Steven would very much like to begin the practice of receiving Holy Communion daily. However, he hesitates because of the many venial sins he commits day after day. Should this keep Dick from receiving Holy Communion daily? Discuss. How can Dick greatly overcome these defects?*

Dick certainly should not allow his venial sins to keep him from receiving daily Holy Communion. The state of sanctifying grace is the only spiritual requirement necessary for the reception of this Holy Sacrament. Anyone who possesses sanctifying grace can increase it in his soul by the frequent reception of Holy Communion. No matter how many venial sins one commits, they alone cannot take away sanctifying grace and hence should not keep one away from Communion. Here again we must remember that we receive Holy Communion not because we are worthy but to help us become worthy. Dick will find that the best means of overcoming his defects lies in the very means he hesitates to use often. By frequent confession and daily Communion he can surely rid himself of his faults and grow to a close union with Christ.

8. *On a questionnaire of a certain men's college, they were asked "to please state frankly your own experience with frequent Communion." Here are some of the frank statements:*

"I seldom if ever commit a mortal sin on the days on which I receive Holy Communion. If I stay away from the sacraments for several days I usually fall into many and grievous sins."

"When I am receiving frequently, I am a soldier; when I am not, I am a moral traitor."

"I cannot do without it now, I actually feel a physical difference when I neglect it for a morning. Yet all the time I am battling rotten desires."

"I have received so many favors and such consolation from the

practice that I feel that the old saying is true: 'God can get along without you, but you cannot get along without God.' "

Would it not be possible for you to go to Holy Communion weekly? Daily?

Many others have found that the sacrifice necessary to receive daily Communion is repaid a hundredfold. No one should deprive himself without necessity of this wonderful life-giving Sacrament. One who realizes the greatness of this Holy Sacrament can nearly always find a way to receive it daily, or at least weekly.

31.

CONFIRMATION

Problem Questions, Chap. XXXVI, pp. 326, 327.

1. *Mr. Smith is a convert. He cannot understand why confirmation is necessary, and therefore, constantly puts it off until next year. Is he guilty of sin? Why is he especially in need of the sacrament of confirmation?*

Mr. Smith, in constantly putting off receiving the sacrament of confirmation when he has had the opportunity of receiving it, is surely committing sin. By so doing he ignores the great use of this sacrament, and especially does he fail to guard himself against the many dangers to faith and morals. All Catholics have great need of the strengthening effects of this sacrament. But Mr. Smith, being a convert, has a special need, because his faith has not had the continued nourishment of the sacraments from childhood as in the case of persons who have been Catholics all their lives.

2. *John Williams was to be confirmed Pentecost afternoon. He went to confession the day before and intended to receive Holy Communion the next morning. Sunday morning, however, John thoughtlessly took a drink of water. May John be confirmed? Why?*

John may be confirmed because the reception of Holy Communion before the reception of the sacrament of confirmation, while a common practice and very praiseworthy, is not strictly necessary for the worthy receiving of the sacrament. If a person has been baptized and is in the state of grace, he may receive confirmation worthily.

3. *Bill Fox was confirmed last Tuesday afternoon but had not heeded the priest's advice to go to confession the day before. Now, two Sundays ago, Bill went fishing and had deliberately not attended Mass. Did Bill receive the sacrament of confirmation? Explain. Of what sins is he guilty? Why?*

Yes, when Bill was confirmed by the bishop he really received the sacrament of confirmation, even though he was not in the state of grace, although he received the sacrament unworthily and committed a grave sin in doing so, Bill will not have to receive the sacrament again because being a baptized person he received the sacrament validly and also the character, regardless of his state of soul at the time.

Bill is guilty of two grave sins. He is guilty of a mortal sin for deliberately failing to attend Mass on Sunday, and he is also guilty of sacrilege in receiving the sacrament of confirmation in a state of mortal sin.

4. *Ray Crowley was confirmed because his friends urged him to be, but before the ceremonies Ray said to himself, "I'll just go through with it for their sakes." Did he receive the sacrament of confirmation? Explain.*

Ray did not receive the sacrament of confirmation because an adult person must have some intention of really receiving the sacrament in order to receive it validly. In deciding "just to go through with it for their sakes," Ray apparently had no intention or desire to receive the sacrament itself, and in such a state could not be validly confirmed.

5. *Shirley Bolley had been given three names in baptism and refused to take another in confirmation. Discuss.*

Shirley need not worry about taking another name in confirmation, because that is not necessary if she does not wish it. It is the usual thing and is a laudable custom inasmuch as it gives one the help and example of another patron saint, but it is not a necessary part of the sacrament. Shirley may present to the bishop on confirmation day any one of the three names she received in baptism, if she does not care to select a new one.

6. *On Albert Barton's confirmation day the street car was delayed by a snowstorm and so he was late. He came into Church just after the bishop's first prayer and imposition of hands. Did he receive the sacrament of confirmation? Explain.*

Yes, Albert received the sacrament of confirmation. The first prayer and imposition of hands occurs in the first part of the confirmation ceremony, when the bishop stands at the altar with his hands extended over the group to be confirmed, and prays that they may receive the Holy Ghost with His sevenfold gifts. It is a very important part of the confirmation ceremony, but the presence of a person at it is not absolutely necessary in order that he receive the sacrament validly. While it is not allowable for anyone to be confirmed to absent himself from this first imposition of hands, it was unavoidable in Albert's case; he was validly confirmed as long as he received the essential part of the sacrament, that is, the individual imposition of hands and anointing by the bishop who at the same time says. "I sign thee with the sign of the cross, and I confirm thee with the chrism of salvation; in the name of the Father, and of the Son, and of the Holy Ghost. Amen."

7. *Mary Lee fainted just after the priest had wiped the chrism from her forehead. She was carried out of church and was unable to return for the last solemn blessing. Has she received the sacrament of confirmation? Explain.*

Yes, Mary Lee certainly received the sacrament of confirmation because her fainting came after the essential part of the sacrament had been conferred. After the bishop had spoken the words of confirmation while anointing her, Mary Lee's presence at the ceremony was no longer strictly necessary.

8. In China, Father Henry confers the sacrament of confirmation. Why can he administer this sacrament?

We say that the bishop is the ordinary minister of the sacrament of confirmation. However, under certain conditions such as exist in missionary countries, the pope may and sometimes does delegate to an ordinary priest the power to administer this sacrament. In this case, the priest is the extraordinary minister of the sacrament, taking the place of the bishop because of the difficulty of travel, the great number of persons to be confirmed, etc. This is the reason Father Henry, in China, is able to confer the sacrament of confirmation.

9. In the bishop's sermon on William's confirmation day, the bishop said to those who were confirmed "Now you are soldiers of Christ." What did he mean?

When William's bishop said, "Now you are soldiers of Christ," he meant: "You who are now about to begin the battle of life — the battle against sin, temptation, assaults on your faith, ridicule of your love for Christ — have received this sacrament which our Lord instituted to give you special strength in this battle. The Holy Ghost has come to you, and if you have received Him worthily, He will in some degree change you as He changed the Apostles. When you were younger you were children of God, but now you are enlisted in the ranks of Christ's soldiers, fighting for Him, now and forever doing the will of Him, your Divine Commander."

32.

MATRIMONY

Problem Question, Chap. XXXVII, p. 333.

1. When fourteen years of age, Marie Carron was very ill with a lingering illness. After a long deliberation and prayer she vowed to enter a religious order should she recover. Marie got well and later felt sorry for having made the vow because she wished to marry. What should Marie do? Discuss Marie's vow.

Marie should consult her confessor. He either possesses or

can readily obtain from the bishop the power to dispense her absolutely from her vow, if it were indeed binding. A vow is a very serious thing, and should be made only when a person is in full possession of his or her powers of mind and body. Marie's mental and physical condition due to her long illness, considered together with her extreme youth, suggest a moral incapacity for making a vow. Besides, her motive was not the best: she seemed to think of the vow as the lesser of two evils.

2. *From childhood Joe Segers said when it came for him to marry he would not have the banns of matrimony published because he disliked the publicity. Why does the Church insist upon the publication of the banns? If necessary, how may one be excused from the publication of the banns?*

The Church so insists to safeguard the sanctity of the sacrament of matrimony. The purpose of the "banns" is to assure the pastor that there exists no impediment which would render the proposed marriage either null (invalid) or illicit (unlawful). A grave obligation binds the faithful to make known to the pastor the existence of any such impediment (such, for example, as would exist should one of the parties be already married). In cases of necessity the bishop may excuse from the law requiring publication of the "banns." Application for such a dispensation should be made to him through the pastor.

3. *After careful consideration and much prayer, Louise Koch and Leonard Neil present themselves before the priest to take each other, "to have and to hold, from this day forward, for better, for worse, for richer, for poorer, in sickness, and in health" until death doth them part. Who administers the sacrament of matrimony? Explain. For how long do Louise and Leonard promise to be faithful to each other?*

Louise and Leonard administer the sacrament to themselves. As a general rule the minister of the sacrament is the person who pronounces the words of the "form." The words, "I do," expressing mutual consent which constitutes the essence of this sacrament, are its "form." And the pronouncing of this "form"

by each party in turn makes them the ministers of the sacrament
They promise mutual fidelity until death separates them.

4. Mr. and Mrs. Borden had been married ten years when suddenly Mr. Borden became a raving maniac. Mrs. Borden had four children for whom it was very difficult to provide. A very favorable opportunity for a second marriage offered itself to Mrs. Borden and she desired to marry since there was no hope for her husband's recovery. May Mrs. Borden obtain a divorce and remarry? Discuss. When does the Church permit separation? Under what conditions may a Catholic be married a second time?

Mrs. Borden may not obtain a divorce and remarry because she is bound by the bond of her first marriage until her husband dies. The existence of this bond constitutes a nullifying (diriment) impediment which would render any attempt at another marriage worthless in the eyes of God and the Church.

The Church (the bishop) may permit a *separation* in any of the following cases:

1) If one party is guilty of adultery, and the other will not be reconciled.

2) If one party apostatizes or embraces a heretical religion.

3) If living together exposes one party to grave danger of soul or body.

4) If one party leads a very sinful life.

5) If both parties, prompted by a good reason, mutually consent to a separation.

As a general rule a Catholic may marry a second time only when his former consort is dead. There are, however, a few rare cases when a Catholic may obtain permission to remarry even while the partner to his first marriage is still alive. Such permission is given by a special ecclesiastical court.

33.

EXTREME UNCTION

Problem Questions, Chap. XXXVIII, p. 339.

1. *Arleen Kelley's father died some years ago. Her father was very ill and no hope of recovery was entertained. She notified their pastor and her brother went to bring him. While waiting for the priest she covered a small table with a white linen cloth, placed a crucifix between two candles, and arranged a glass of water, a bottle of holy water, a napkin, five little balls of cotton, and a little piece of bread neatly on the table. When the priest came, Arleen met him at the door with a lighted candle, for she knew her father was to receive Viaticum also. For a little while they left their father alone with the priest while he made his last confession. Her father then received the Holy Viaticum. After a few prayers and a few words of consolation, the priest took the oils he had brought with him and made the sign of the cross on the dying man's eyes, ears, nose, lips, hands, and feet while he repeated the prayer, "Through this Holy Unction and His most tender mercy may the Lord forgive thee whatever sins thou hast committed by sight, hearing," etc.*

What is the purpose of each article Arleen placed upon the table? What is the meaning of the oil used in administering the sacrament of extreme unction? Why does the priest anoint the five sense organs? What is the meaning of the prayer the priest says while anointing each member? Why should one, if possible, go to bring the priest?

a) The white linen cloth serves as an altar cloth, for the table is to become a small altar. The crucifix and candles must adorn an altar on which the Blessed Sacrament is to be exposed. The crucifix is given to the dying person to gaze at and kiss. This excites love of our Lord and sorrow for sins. The priest will use the water to purify his fingers after he has given Holy Communion to the sick person. With the holy water the priest sprinkles the patient, the family, and the sickroom immediately upon his arrival. On the napkin the priest dries his hands. The balls of cotton are used to wipe the holy oil off the sick man's organs after they have been anointed. The priest uses the piece of bread to wipe the holy oil from his own fingers. The cotton, the bread, and the water in which the priest purified his hands are to be thrown into the stove or furnace and burned. If this is not convenient the priest must take them with him and dispose of them himself.

b) Oil has always been used to strengthen the human body. The ancient wrestlers rubbed themselves with it, and athletes still use it to make their muscles supple and strong while doctors prescribe it as an aid in the building up of strong, healthy children (cod-liver oil). The Church has taken over the practice of anointing with oil and uses it as the symbol or outward sign of the spiritual strength imparted to the soul by the sacrament. This anointing is thus symbolically used in baptism, confirmation (I confirm thee with the Chrism of salvation), holy orders, and extreme unction.

c) The five senses are the chief instruments whereby man sins.

d) The prayer entreats God to forgive — through the merits of the grace of this sacrament — all the sins committed by the use or abuse of the several senses.

e) It will enable the priest to come more quickly, he will not have to find his way. Besides, the person calling for the priest can give him necessary information about the condition, age, dispositions, etc., of the sick person. Then too, the Blessed Sacrament is worthy of the special protection and honor a man accompanying the priest would offer.

2. Some people have a false notion about the reception of extreme unction. They think that when one has received the sacrament of extreme unction he is sure to die, or that the priest is called when death is certain. What is the purpose of the sacrament?

All the sacraments were instituted by Christ to fulfill a certain definite purpose, and it would contradict the infinite wisdom and power of God if these sacraments effected something directly opposite to that for which they were instituted. Now, Extreme Unction was instituted to give health and strength (both physical, if God so wills, and spiritual) to sick people. So it could not possibly cause people to die. This false notion is perpetuated because some Catholics wrongly wait until a person is almost dead before they summon the priest. Such delay is wrong and often dangerous. The priest should be summoned as soon as the physician says or circumstances indicate that the patient is seriously ill. An even better rule might be: when anyone is sick enough to have the doctor, he or she should also have the priest.

3. *A person feels great peace and joy after receiving the sacrament of extreme unction. This is clear to every member of his family. What is one of the effects of the sacrament of extreme unction? Why is a holy person sometimes filled with anxiety on his deathbed?*

a) The sacrament has the effect of banishing from the soul that dread and horror with which the thought of death naturally fills it, and of replacing this dread with a sense of heavenly peace and comfort based on trust in God's goodness and mercy and on resignation to His holy will.

b) (1) A holy person has a deeper knowledge and realization of the heinousness of sin and the enormity of its offense against God. (2) The devil always tempts and torments holy people more than ordinary (e.g., the Curé of Ars). And in this case the evil one hopes by suggesting the greatness of the sins committed by the sick person to plunge him into despair.

4. *All hope for the recovery of Roger Stanton had been lost. The priest was called, and immediately after the administration of the sacrament of extreme unction a decided change in the patient was noticeable. Roger did not die, but a change for the better took place and it was a matter of only a few weeks before Roger was around again. What is another effect of the sacrament of extreme unction? Why is it foolish to think that death is absolutely imminent when the sacrament of extreme unction is administered?*

a) To restore to health if God sees fit.

b) As explained above in Problem 2, death can never be attributed to the sacrament. From a purely natural and physical point of view extreme unction consists simply in the application of a bit of oil to the senses. This surely could not cause death. This superstitious attitude must be dissipated. From the psychological viewpoint the patient should, and generally does, feel better after receiving the sacrament. A worrisome burden is lifted from his mind, and with it disappears its corresponding physical strain, so that now the vital forces can apply themselves unhindered to the work of fighting the sickness. (Worry impedes the proper work of the blood, etc., as, for example, in the matter of digestion.)

34.

HOLY ORDERS

Problem Questions, Chap. XXXIX, p. 347.

1. *In the Old Testament God chose the Levites to carry on the priestly duties among His people. At the Last Supper, Christ established the priesthood when He consecrated the Apostles to their work in the words: "Do this for a commemoration of Me"; and after His Resurrection: "Receive ye the Holy Ghost, whose sins you shall forgive they are forgiven them, whose sins you shall retain they are retained." Who has the power to ordain? Discuss the Apostolic succession. What is the sacrament of holy orders?*

The bishops being the successors of the Apostles have the power to ordain.

"Apostolic succession is the uninterrupted succession of lawfully ordained bishops extending from the Apostles down to the present bishops of the Church, who thus have received the powers of ordaining, ruling, and teaching bestowed on the Apostles by Christ" (*Catholic Dictionary*). Apostolic succession does not mean that specific bishops are successors of specific Apostles. It means that all the bishops taken collectively are the successors of the College of Apostles. Because the Church was not to end with the death of Christ He appointed the Apostles; because it was not to end with the last of the Apostles, it was necessary for the Apostles to ordain men to succeed them, men who would perpetuate the same mission given them by Christ. So while the Apostles were yet living they appointed and ordained men. In some churches one was established as bishop to care for the church in the absence of the Apostle and to succeed him when he died. Thus, in the second century it was certain that the general Apostolic authority belonged, by a succession universally recognized as legitimate, to the bishops of the Christian Churches. A permanent episcopate, under the headship of Peter, was founded by Christ on His Apostles who passed on their mission to legitimately ordained successors. That this succession has continued unbroken until now is a fact of history. If a break has occurred in the past, a fact of so great importance would have attracted universal notice.

Holy Orders is a sacrament of the New Law, instituted by Christ, by which bishops, priests, and other ministers of the Church are ordained and receive the power and the grace to perform their sacred duties.

2. *Charles Coele had heard of the coming ordination of John McMahoney and out of mere curiosity made arrangements to attend. During the ceremony the bishop and the priests first imposed hands upon John. Then the bishop anointed the young man's hands with holy oils and gave him the chalice with wine and the paten with a host saying at the same time: "Receive the power to offer sacrifice to God and to celebrate Mass." Lastly, the bishop placed his hands a second time on John's head and said: "Receive the Holy Ghost, whose sins you shall forgive they are forgiven them, and whose sins you shall retain they are retained." What is the meaning of each step in the process of ordination? Why is holy orders called the sacrament of the Holy Ghost? What is the preparation for the sacrament of holy orders?*

The imposition of hands during the ceremony signifies that something is given, since gifts are distributed with the hands.

That which is given is the power of the priesthood. In Apostolic times the imposition of hands constituted the whole ordination ceremony. By it there was conferred not only the powers of the priesthood but also the grace necessary for the office. "I admonish thee, that thou stir up the grace of God which is in thee through the imposition of hands" (II Tim. i. 6).

The hands of the young man were anointed with holy oils to signify that they are consecrated to God, since they are the means by which the Holy Sacrifice of the Mass is offered to God. They are also the means by which all things are blessed.

The young man was given the chalice with wine and the paten with the host because these are the vessels and the objects used in the Holy Sacrifice of the Mass.

The touching of the chalice and paten occurs simultaneously with the words of the bishop: "Receive the power to offer sacrifice to God and to celebrate Mass as well for the living as for the dead." By this ceremony the young man receives the power of celebrating Mass.

The second imposition of hands signifies that another power is given. Because of the excellence of the power to forgive sins, a special ceremony is employed to express its bestowal upon the priest. The bishop imposes hands and says: "Receive ye the Holy Ghost; whose sins you shall forgive they are forgiven them, and whose sins you shall retain they are retained." Immediately the young man is invested with the divine power of forgiving and retaining sins, the power which our Lord conferred on His Apostles on Easter Sunday morning.

Holy Orders may be called the sacrament of the Holy Ghost because at the imposition of hands the Holy Ghost is conferred in a special manner (*Cath. Ency.*, Art. "Orders").

Preparation for the sacrament of Holy Orders — cf. pp. 343, 344, Text.

35.

PRAYER

Problem Questions, Chap. XL, p. 356.

1. *Is prayer a source of grace? What is the other principal source of grace?*

Prayer is indeed an important source of grace because it is by this means that we become properly disposed to receive supernatural gifts from God, and because God wills that those to whom he gives grace shall ask for it. The other principal source of grace is the sacraments.

2. *To whom should we pray?*

We should pray to God; Father, Son, and Holy Ghost. God must be the ultimate object of all our prayers since He is the only one to whom we owe adoration; Him we must thank who is the author of all good, to Him we must make reparation for our sins, and to Him we must direct all our petitions. In other words, all that we are and all that we have or shall have comes from God; and the most efficacious communication between ourselves and God is prayer.

3. *To whom should we pray for intercession?*

We can most profitably pray to the blessed in heaven for intercession; namely, the Blessed Virgin, the angels, the saints, and even the souls in purgatory. All of these have proved their friendship for God, and by honoring them we honor God who will readily grant those requests for which the saints, His friends, intercede on our behalf.

151

4. *Why is the "Our Father" a perfect prayer?*

The Our Father is a perfect prayer, first, because it was given to us by our Lord at the request of the Apostles that He teach them to pray. Hence we must assume that Jesus would give them a most fitting prayer. Secondly, it is perfectly designed to express man's sentiments toward God. Finally, its perfection is seen in this that it expresses our own needs and desires in a most fitting manner.

5. *Tell the parable of the Pharisee and the Publican. What does it suggest to us about our own prayer?*

Two men went up to the Temple to pray; one was a Pharisee and the other a Publican. The Pharisee standing prayed thus with himself: "O God, I give Thee thanks that I am not as the rest of men, extortioners, unjust, adulterers, as also is this Publican. I fast twice a week, I give tithes of all that I possess." And the Publican standing afar off would not so much as lift up his eyes toward heaven; but struck his breast saying: "O God, be merciful to me a sinner" (Luke xviii. 10–13). From this parable we learn that our prayers must not be proud and boastful but rather humble and sincere.

6. *What is mental prayer?*

Mental prayer is the raising of our hearts and minds to God — without this expression of our sentiments being in any verbal form. It is the contemplation of God in His attributes or in His works, and the adoration of His Goodness and Omnipotence. Meditation may also have for its object the life of Christ, the mysteries of our religion, or the lives of the saints insofar as they mirror forth the perfections of the Creator. In fine, it is the use of the imagination, memory, and intellect to effect a communion with God without employing verbal expression. This is mental prayer or meditation strictly so called. Verbal prayer, on the other hand, must include some intellectual attention lest there be only empty words. These two forms of prayer may very properly go hand in hand — as in the case of the Rosary where we meditate on the mysteries while saying the Our Father and Hail Mary. Furthermore, in formal meditation the introduction of frequent verbal aspirations is to be recommended.

7. *Name the characteristics of prayer.*

Prayer should have the following characteristics or qualities to make it a worthy mode of communication with God.

The first characteristic is attention. By this is meant that our thoughts are directed to God and that our sentiments correspond to the substance of the prayer. Since prayer is essentially "speaking to God" it is only fitting that we be attentive to what we are saying. This may be illustrated by the fact that when we are speaking seriously to any person we pay attention to the manner in which we suit the words to the thought we wish to express; otherwise, we speak foolishly and the listener cannot understand us. How much more ought we be recollected when speaking to God.

Secondly, prayer must be humble. If we realize to whom we are speaking, we may well wonder how we dare to utter even a word. Yet He has told us to pray; hence we speak humbly, conscious of our nothingness and of our dependence on God who created us and who preserves us in all our actions and in our very existence. We abandon ourselves to God's goodness, knowing that His answer to our prayer will be in a way that is best for us.

The third characteristic of prayer is confidence. We firmly trust that God will hear and answer our prayers. We remember that He has said that if we have sufficient faith we can move mountains. We know that God is all powerful and all wise, and that nothing is too great for Him to do — provided that it will be good for us.

"All things whatsoever you shall ask in prayer, believing, you shall receive" (Matt. xxi. 22).

Perseverance is the fourth quality of prayer. This simply means not being discouraged if our prayers seem to bring no reply but rather praying the harder to assure God of our conformity to His Will.

Finally we should pray *"Through Jesus Christ Our Lord."* In the official prayers of the Church and especially in the Mass, prayers are offered to God through Christ our Mediator.

8. *Write a prayer to God for your spiritual welfare.*

O Almighty and Eternal God, my Creator, Preserver and Redeemer and the source of all blessings, consider not my unworthiness but through the merits of Christ Thy Son, the Blessed Virgin Mary, and the saints, protect me from all evil that may beset my soul and endanger my salvation. Grant me Thy divine assistance so to live that I may do Thy will in all things and thereby honor Thee and obtain my salvation. Amen.

9. *Write a prayer for your mother. Your father.*

O my God, who in Thy goodness hast placed me upon this earth and hast given me for my guidance and example a good and virtuous mother, grant that her many acts of love and sacrifice may be united to those of the Blessed Mother of Thy Son for Thy honor and glory and for her spiritual and temporal welfare through the same Christ Thy Son. Amen.

My Lord and Savior, Jesus Christ, who taught us to pray "Our Father," by the love Thou dost bear Thy Divine Father and by the respect Thou didst show Thy Foster-father, St. Joseph, grant to my earthly father peace of soul and Thy blessing on his untiring efforts to serve Thee and the family Thou hast given him. May his days spent in doing Thy holy will merit for him eternal happiness in the kingdom of Thy Father. Amen.

10. *Write a prayer for the welfare of the United States.*

O Immaculate Mother Mary, patroness of these United States, who art ever mindful of those under your special protection, continue to beg the mercy of thy Divine Son in our behalf, and implant in the hearts of the citizens of this bountiful land a respect for the representatives of God's will both in Church and State. Free the hearts of those who govern from the bondage of sin, that serving God in all truth and justice, this nation may be found pleasing in His sight from whom comes all blessings and all power. Grant that the Church and State in this land may work together in directing the people along the path of temporal and spiritual prosperity, and that charity and faith in Christ may be the universal motives of our patriotism.

11. *Write a prayer that you may find in life its joyousness as St. Francis of Assisi did.*

O dear Jesus, Creator of this beautiful world, permit us to see in every object, be it tree, bird, stone, or fellow man, the reflection of Thy goodness and Thy will. May it be our joy to live in this habitation, which Thou hast provided for us, in a spirit of good will toward all; and to serve Thee, our Kind Master, until Thou shalt call us to the greater joys of Paradise where we shall see Thee, the Font of Joy, face to face. Amen.

12. *Write a morning prayer. An evening prayer.*

Morning Prayer: O Jesus, through the Immaculate Heart of Mary, I offer Thee my prayers, works, and sufferings of this day for all the intentions of Thy Sacred Heart in union with the Holy Sacrifice of the Mass throughout the world for the intentions of all my friends, relations, and benefactors, and in particular for the salvation of my immortal soul. (Apostleship of Prayer.)

Evening Prayer: I cast myself on my knees before Thee, O Lord, at the end of this day, I adore Thee because Thou art all good and holy, I thank Thee for the many graces received from Thy bountiful hands today, I ask pardon for all my sins, offenses, and negligences by which I have turned from Thee. I ask for Your merciful protection during this coming night and the grace to live another day to serve Thee and to repair for my sins. Amen.

13. *Find a liturgical morning prayer. A liturgical evening prayer.*

Liturgical Morning Prayer: O Almighty God, who hast brought us into another day, may we by virtue of Thy saving graces be strengthened against all sin and walk in the way of Thy justice and love, in all our thoughts, words, and actions. Through our Lord Jesus Christ forever. Amen. (The Breviary.)

Evening Prayer: Let us pray: visit, we beg Thee, O Lord, this house and keep from it all the influence of the evil one; may Thy holy angels dwell herein to guard our peace and may Thy blessings be upon us this night and forever, through Christ our Lord. Amen. (The Breviary.)

14. *What is meant by Matins, Lauds, Prime, Terce, Sext, None, Vespers, and Compline.*

Matins, Lauds, Prime, Terce, Sext, None, Vespers, and Compline are the names of the prayer hours of the day. The daily prayers are thus divided in the Breviary, the official prayer book of the Church. These prayers are read by every priest. They are chanted in the chapels of monasteries, seminaries, and convents.

15. *Are there spiritual exercises for the soul just as there are physical exercises for the body? If so, name them.*

The Spiritual Exercises of St. Ignatius of Loyola were designed by their author to strengthen the soul in the spiritual life in much the same way as physical exercises strengthen man in his bodily life.

16. *Find out what you can about the life of St. Ignatius of Loyola at Manresa.*

After his conversion from a rather wayward life as a soldier in the Spanish army, St. Ignatius turned his back on the world and set out to devote the rest of his life to the saving of his soul. With this in mind he sold all earthly goods and retired to a cave near the town of Manresa, in Spain, in 1522. Here he prayed, fasted, and did penance for his sins. God tried His servant with many crosses and temptations. After having triumphed over all these obstacles, he began to make notes of his spiritual experiences. These revised notes became the famous Spiritual Exercises.

17. *Find out what you can about the Spiritual Exercises of St. Ignatius of Loyola.*

They consist mainly in developing strong convictions which rid the soul of sin and build up a resistance to all evil inclinations. By prayer and meditation the exercises lead a person to dispose himself as a soldier of Christ in the battle of life against Satan and the powers of darkness.

18. *What is a retreat?*

A retreat is a "going apart from the things of the world to contemplate the eternal truths concerning God and self." A retreat, in its most usual form, is a certain time spent in seclusion from temporal considerations and devoted to a "spiritual inventory"; in it the soul is free to think and pray and thereby bring itself into the proper dispositions of Christian living. Ordinarily the retreatant is under the direction of a spiritual guide who leads him along a gradual ascent, from the things which take our attention from God, to those things which unite us to Him.

36.

COMMANDMENTS OF THE CHURCH

Problem Questions, Chap. XLI, pp. 365, 366.

1. *Roy Chanders, a Protestant friend of yours, says, "The Catholic Church has no right to command you under pain of mortal sin to attend Mass on Sundays and Holydays of Obligation." From whence does the Catholic Church get its authority? Why does the Church command one to attend Mass on these days? Summarize the arguments to clear up Roy's objections.*

The Catholic Church receives its authority from Jesus Christ. While Christ lived on earth He founded the Church, gave to it His authority, and left it here below to take His place. Our Lord promised that He Himself would be with His Church until the end of time and that He would send the Holy Ghost, the Paraclete, to abide in the Church and guide it in the way of truth. The Church acts in Christ's Name, and will continue to effect His will among all peoples of all times until the end of the world.

The Church, speaking as the representative of Christ, commands us to attend Mass on these days in order to assure our

carrying out of the first and particularly the third commandments of God. By obeying the Church's law on hearing Mass,
we carry out God's commandment in the way ordained for us
by Christ through His visible representative, the Church. Our
Lord instituted the Sacrifice of the Mass that we might worship
God, our Creator, in a way infinitely more perfect than the
worship of the pagans and Jews. We are commanded to assist
at Mass: (1) on all Sundays of the year; it was on a Sunday
that Christ rose from the dead and that the Holy Ghost came
upon the Apostles; (2) on certain other days called Holydays
of Obligation, which commemorate the great mysteries of our
religion and the virtues and rewards of the saints. If we refuse
to obey the Church which Christ left to guide and help us on
the Highway to God, we disobey God, show contempt for our
Lord, and certainly commit grievous sin.

2. *"I am going to Church today, Mother, just to hear the music
and to hear Father Smith speak," said Rita Bailey as she left
home one Sunday morning. Does Rita Bailey fulfill her duty of
hearing Mass? Explain. Why is bodily presence not enough to
fulfill the obligation of hearing Mass? How would the situation
differ if Rita went to Church for the purpose of hearing Mass
but read a storybook during the entire service?*

Rita Bailey does not fulfill her obligation of hearing Sunday
Mass if she goes solely to hear the music and the sermon. The
obligation of hearing Mass on Sundays and Holydays is placed
upon us that we may fulfill our obligation of giving worship to
Almighty God. In order to do that, we must not only be bodily
present at the Mass, but we must have some sort of intention of
performing a religious act, of giving honor to God in some way
other than by our mere bodily presence. If we went to Mass for
other reasons and with no intention of worshiping God by some
kind of religious assistance, we should certainly not fulfill the
First Commandment of the Church.

If Rita went to Church for the purpose of hearing Mass but
read a storybook during the entire time of Mass, she would in-

deed have the *intention* of religious assistance, but she would lack the necessary *attention,* which means the occupying of our time in Church as far as possible in a religious way, that is, reading of the Mass prayers, saying or reading other prayers, etc. If a person spent all the time in Church doing something in no way connected with the worship of God, he would fail in the attention required for a religious act and would not satisfy his obligation of hearing Mass.

3. *Bernard Quinn went to Church on a Sunday morning with the intention of hearing Mass. He was out late the evening before, and so fell asleep soon after Mass had begun and did not wake up until the Communion of the Mass. Did Bernard fulfill his duty? Discuss. Why does the Church exhort the faithful not to attend late Saturday night functions? When may a person be excused from hearing Mass?*

In sleeping through the Mass until the Communion, Bernard failed to fulfill his duty of hearing Mass. Assistance at Mass required to fulfill one's obligation consists of more than mere physical presence in the church; one must also be occupied in a religious way during the time of Mass. In spite of his good intention, Bernard slept through the most important part of the Mass and surely could not be said to have "heard Mass." While he had the proper intention, he lacked the *attention* necessary to fulfill his obligation.

It is in order to prevent cases like that of Bernard that the Church exhorts the faithful not to attend late Saturday night functions. A person who knowingly and unnecessarily tires himself so greatly as to interfere with his hearing of Sunday Mass, certainly does not show the proper attitude toward the worship of God, acts contrary to the spirit of Christ and the Church, and stands in danger of sinning gravely.

A person may be excused from hearing Mass for certain grave reasons:

(1) When it is *impossible* for him to come because of infirmity, sickness, great distance from the Church, or without great loss of money, etc.

(2) When *charity* toward one's neighbor demands one's presence, as in the case of a sick person with no one to care for him.

(3) When the *duties* of one's state in life prevent one from attending Mass, as in the case of nurses, soldiers, sailors, etc.

4. *One Sunday morning Betty's mother was ready to go to Mass, when she heard that a neighbor was very ill and needed help. Instead of going to church she went to help the neighbor. Did she do right?*

Betty's mother did quite right in going to help her neighbor as long as there was no one else who could aid the sick person. As we have seen, the need of helping a neighbor is one of the reasons which excuses one from missing Mass.

5. *Marie was out to a dance all Saturday night. She was very tired on Sunday morning, but decided to go to Mass before returning home. She slept all during the services. Did she fulfill her obligation to hear a Mass?*

Like Bernard Quinn who slept through most of the Mass, Marie failed to fulfill her obligation when she slept through the entire Mass. Saturday night dances which keep one from fulfilling his duties toward God should most certainly be avoided.

6. *There was no school on the Feast of Corpus Christi and John and William decided to go fishing. John thought that the feast was a holyday of obligation, but he did not attend Mass. Afterwards he heard from William that he was not obliged to hear a Mass on that day, as it was not a holyday of obligation. John said he was glad to hear that, for now he did not commit a mortal sin by not attending Mass. William said it would be a sin for John anyway, because he had thought that it was a sin when he decided to stay away. Who was right, and why?*

William was right in saying John committed sin by not attending Mass on a day he thought was a holyday, because the malice or badness of a sin lies in the intention of doing it. A person thereby turns away from what he thinks to be right and refuses to do the will of God. John committed sin by making up his mind to do what he thought was wrong. His sin was one of evil intention. His discovering later that Corpus Christi was not a holyday of obligation did not change the nature of his previous decision to do what he considered was wrong.

7. *Mr. Peale is a Catholic. He goes to Mass on All Saints' Day but refuses to let his servants go as they are being paid for their work. Has he a right to keep them from hearing a Mass?*

Mr. Peale has no right to prevent his servants from going to Mass even though they are paid for their work. The law of the Church commands Catholics to be present at Mass themselves, and also not to prevent or hinder others under their charge from attending Mass unless there is a grave reason for such action. Mr. Peale's Catholic sense should tell him that the worship of Almighty God is more important than the slight loss possibly occasioned by his servants' absence during the short time required for Mass. In an unusual circumstance when the absence of the servants would be the cause of grave loss to Mr. Peale, his action might be justified.

8. *On Sunday afternoon you get a big tear in your coat. You need your coat on Monday morning. May mother mend it for you?*

Mother may certainly mend your coat on Sunday in a case like this, because it is necessary to do so. God does not demand the unreasonable of us. On Sundays we should attend Mass and endeavor to observe the spirit of the third commandment. Then, as we have learned, work is lawful when the honor of God, the good of our neighbor, or necessity require them.

9. *Mr. Mack works in an office and cannot get to Mass on the Feast of the Assumption unless he rises at 4:30. Is he obliged to hear Mass?*

Yes, Mr. Mack is obliged to hear Mass on the Feast of the Assumption. The hardship of early rising on a rare occasion like this hardly creates an impossibility or a really serious reason for missing so important an act of our religion.

The Mass is the most sublime of all religious actions. It is the highest expression of the honor which every man owes to God. One who appreciates this sufficiently will gladly sacrifice something of his own comfort in order to participate in the Mass at least on the days of obligation. Mr. Mack would be excused only if rising at 4:30 would seriously interfere with his health or work.

10. *May you stay away from Mass on Sunday because you have a slight headache? a toothache? because you cannot find your Sunday hat?*

No, you may not stay away from Mass because of a slight headache or toothache. Attendance at Mass in such cases might be a bit uncomfortable but certainly would not endanger one's health in any way. Nor would inability to find one's Sunday hat be a sufficient reason for staying away. There would surely be no great public disgrace in appearing in a weekday hat. Moreover, we should be more concerned with the appearance of our souls in the sight of God than with the correctness of our wardrobe, viewed only by men.

Problem Questions, Chap. XLI, pp. 370–371.

1. *Harvey Hennepin spent his vacation working on the boats. Every Friday meat was served by the steward. Harvey was a practical Catholic and refused to take meat and gravy. Rene Bedard, another Catholic, ate the meat when served. One day the steward said to Harvey "Any time you want fish you can get a can from the shelf."*

"Rene's a Catholic too, so we can have it between us," remarked Harvey.

"Oh, no," said the steward, "Let him go. He eats the meat."

What effect did the Catholic attitude of these boys have upon the steward? Who do you think has the better chance for promotion? Why? Would the boys be obliged to refrain from eating meat aboard the boat? Discuss.

The case of Harvey and Rene shows again that no one likes a weakling or a coward. The Catholic who lives his religion in the face of opposition is always more admired by non-Catholics than is the one who forgets his religion when it is more comfortable to do so. The steward's offer of fish to Harvey shows that he was interested in him and esteemed him highly for his observance of the Commandments of the Church to which he belongs. Harvey would undoubtedly have the better chance for promotion because he showed greater will power and ability to do the right thing even when it is difficult.

The boys would be obliged to see if it were possible to obtain meals without meat on the Fridays while working on the boat. If it were not possible to do so, they would be allowed to eat the meals served on the boat even though they contained meat, for such meals would be their only source of nourishment. Practically, however, in this case — as in most cases — fish was to be had for the asking. By going to only a bit of extra trouble one could both obey the law of the Church and avoid giving scandal to non-Catholics.

2. Mr. Kendall, a Catholic, was looking for work in a large city. He did not have a penny left and was obliged to beg for food. On a Friday he was given a meat sandwich. May Mr. Kendall eat the meat sandwich? How would the situation differ if he were not in great need of food? When you are traveling may you eat meat on Friday? Discuss.

Mr. Kendall would be quite right in eating the meat sandwich, since the poor are allowed to eat meat given them when they do not have sufficient other food. If Mr. Kendall did not have great need of food, he should try first to obtain something else before eating the meat on Friday.

One who is traveling is not allowed — just because he is traveling — to order meat on Friday. He must first make a serious effort to obtain other food, even if it means some inconvenience If other foods are not to be had, he may then satisfy his hunger by partaking of meat.

3. Bertha Haley is not excused from fasting because of her duties. She, however, feels unable to fast. What should she do? When should this be done? What obligation still rests on those excused from fasting during Lent? Mention three other ways of doing penance. Name six classes of persons who are excused from fasting during Lent.

If Bertha Haley feels unable to fast, she should ask her confessor to dispense her from fasting. This dispensation ought to be obtained before Lent begins.

Those excused from fasting during Lent are obliged to substitute some other form of penance to take the place of fasting. Besides fasting one may do penance by self-denial of other kinds, prayer, and almsgiving.

Six classes of persons who are excused from fasting during Lent are:

1) Those under 21 years of age.
2) Those who have begun their sixtieth year of age.
3) Sick or infirm persons.
4) The poor who at times cannot get sufficient nourishment.
5) Persons with strenuous work or manner of life.
6) Those dispensed from the fast for other reasons.

4. John Cannon refuses to observe the fast and abstinence regulations during the ember weeks because he claims that the Friday abstinence and the Lenten fast are sufficient. Why is John, nevertheless, guilty of sin? Why have the ember weeks' been instituted? At what time of the year do the ember weeks occur?

John is guilty of sin in disregarding the fast and abstinence on ember days because he violates a law of the Church. The laws of a Church on fast and abstinence are made for our own good; they are made by the authority which the Church derives from Christ, and they oblige all Catholics under pain of sin — whether or not one thinks they are useful to him.

The ember weeks have been instituted as times of special prayer and thanksgiving for the prosperity and blessings of the four seasons of the year. They remind us in a particular way of our dependence upon God as His creatures. There is an ember week at the beginning of each season of the year; namely, winter, spring, summer, and autumn.

Problem Questions, Chap. XLI, p. 372.

1. *Mr. Rits, a careless Catholic, wishes to fulfill his Easter duty of receiving the sacraments of penance and of the Holy Eucharist mostly because he is a member of the Catholic Order of Foresters. He knows that if he goes to confession to his pastor he will be severely scolded. Must he confess to his pastor? Discuss. What obligation has he of fulfilling these duties in his parish? What is the penalty of the Catholic Church for those who do not receive these sacraments during the Easter season?*

No, Mr. Rits is not obliged to confess to his pastor. Everyone has absolute freedom of choice in choosing his confessor. At one time it was required to confess in one's own parish, but the Church has abrogated this law. Confession ought now to be easy for everyone, and such a thing as sacrilegious confession ought to be unknown.

While the Church does not at all ask that the obligation of annual confession be fulfilled in one's own parish, she does strongly urge that the faithful fulfill their duty of receiving Holy Eucharist during the Easter time in their own parishes. If one fulfills the obligation in a parish other than his own, he should inform his pastor of the fact, so the pastor will know that the obligation has been fulfilled.

Until a few years ago the penalty of the Church for those who did not fulfill the Easter obligation was excommunication and denial of Christian burial; today this penalty is not applied except in the case of public and manifest sinners. Persons, however, who do not fulfill their Easter obligation, commit mortal sin which will bring about a most serious penalty.

2. In a certain parish, it is very rarely that the penitent has a chance to go to confession to any other priest than the regular pastor. While fulfilling his Easter duty, a certain young man deliberately concealed a mortal sin. On the following morning he received Holy Communion. Discuss from the Easter duty point of view. Why is such conduct the height of folly?

In making a sacrilegious confession the young man committed another mortal sin and did not fulfill his Easter duty. A confession, in which no sins are forgiven but a new mortal sin added to the soul, could scarcely be considered as fulfilling a law which aims at the sanctification of the person confessing. Such conduct is the height of folly because there is no reason whatever for concealing a mortal sin in confession. No matter how bad the sin, it will be forgiven if sincerely confessed; no one will ever know of it, except the priest, who is bound to the strictest secrecy.

3. After a good confession and before receiving Holy Communion: Jack smoked a cigaret; Mary chewed gum; Mr. Jenden took a headache tablet; Some snowflakes blew into Jane's mouth. Discuss each one's case. May they receive? How does the law of fast oblige the sick?

Jack smoked a cigaret; he may go to Holy Communion because smoking is quite a different thing from eating or drinking and does not break one's fast. However, a boy who smokes before Holy Communion does not show a wholly respectful attitude toward his Eucharistic Lord.

Mary chewed gum; she may not receive Holy Communion because fresh gum contains fruit juices of one kind or another, the swallowing of which would break her fast.

Mr. Jenden took a headache tablet; he may not receive Holy Communion because the headache tablet, like all medicine, breaks the fast necessary for the reception of Holy Communion.

Some snowflakes blew into Jane's mouth; she may receive Holy Communion because such very small particles would not break one's fast when swallowed quite accidentally in this way.

The law of fast obliges the sick when they are able to fulfill the law. However, the sick are exempt from the law in two cases. First, when a person is in danger of death he may receive Holy Communion without fasting. Second, a person who has been sick for a month and is without certain hope of a speedy recovery may, with the permission of his confessor, receive Holy Communion once or twice a week, even though he has taken medicine or something to drink beforehand. (Code of Canon Law, Canon 858, Sec. 2; Cardinal Gasparri, *The Catholic Catechism*, Part III, q. 404.)

Problem Questions, Chap. XLI, pp. 373, 374.

1. *Thirty years ago there were no "Stop" and "Go" signals on busy street corners. Can you explain why? What would happen if there were none now? What happens to people who do not obey these signals? Do you think it will ever be necessary to make traffic laws for airplanes? When?*

"Stop and Go" signals were unheard of thirty years ago because there was no need of such a contrivance in the days of the horse and buggy. When vehicles using the street were fewer and much slower there was no great danger of street-corner collisions and hence no great need of the "Stop and Go" signals. These signals are necessary today because traffic conditions have changed almost entirely. With hundreds of automobiles in every city and all of them moving at speeds unknown in the times of the horse and buggy, there would be no end of collisions, pedestrian deaths, and traffic jams if we did not have the order brought about by the "Stop and Go" signals.

Persons who do not obey these signals endanger their own lives and those of other citizens and in that measure commit sin; they are frequently arrested, fined, and sometimes imprisoned.

It seems most reasonable that it will some day be necessary to make traffic laws for airplanes. Although conditions do not demand such regulation right now, airplanes are becoming so numerous that within a very few years it may be necessary to make laws to meet the new condition of a crowded air traffic.

2. The early Christians received Holy Communion every time they went to Mass. Do you think that under those circumstances it was necessary to make a law which obliged them to go to Holy Communion at least once a year? Why not? Why do you suppose the Church had to make such a law later?

In the early centuries of the Church, the Christian people seemed to have a clearer understanding of the sacraments; they received Holy Communion of their own accord practically every time they attended Mass. It is easy to see that there was then no need for a law obliging people to go to Holy Communion at least once a year; they voluntarily went much more frequently than that. There was no need for a law to correct a condition which was already quite satisfactory. Later, however, the attitude in regard to the reception of the sacraments changed; people began to receive Holy Communion less frequently; they grew quite careless in many instances, and thus a new situation arose. It was to correct this new situation and to make sure that all her children would share in the life-giving effects of the Most Holy Sacrament that the Church had to make a law obliging everyone to receive Holy Communion at least once a year.

3. Mr. Goodwin says that there is nothing in the Bible about going to confession or Holy Communion at least once a year. In fact, he points out to you that this law of the Church was made in 1215 and therefore could not have come directly from Christ. What do you say? Look up the Fourth Lateran Council and tell the class what the Church decreed. (The teacher will guide you.)

It is quite true that the Bible in speaking of the forgiveness of sins and the reception of the Eucharist does not command that these sacraments must be received once a year. But the Bible was not written as a complete record of all the truths and laws of the Christian religion. Our Lord did not write down His teachings; He did not found His religion on a book. Christ delegated His work of saving souls to a living society known as His Church. Guided by the Holy Ghost, the Church speaks for Christ. New heresies call for the more specific explanation of religious truths; new conditions in the ever-changing world call for the formulation of more precise laws to direct the souls of the faithful. Thus have come into existence the present-day laws for the reception of the sacraments of penance and Holy Eucharist. If they "do not come directly from Christ," it is because He Himself willed that they should come indirectly — through His Church.

The Fourth Lateran Council, convoked by Pope Innocent III in the year 1215, decreed in its twenty-first canon that everyone of the faithful who has attained the use of reason must confess his sins at least once a year to his own parish priest and receive Holy Eucharist at least during the Paschal season, unless for some good reason the priest thinks the person should wait for a time. This decree is a part of the law of the Church today except that it is not now required to make the annual confession to one's own parish priest. (Cf. Art., "Lateran Councils," *Cath. Ency.,* Vol. IX, p. 18.)

4. *Mr. Blake goes to confession and Holy Communion once a year at Christmas time. Does he fulfill his obligation in regard to the third commandment of the Church? To the fourth?*

In going to confession and Holy Communion once a year at Christmas time, Mr. Blake fulfills the third commandment of the Church; the third commandment of the Church does not specify when the required yearly confession must be made. Mr. Blake does not, however, fulfill the fourth commandment of the Church, which states that the Holy Eucharist is to be received during the Easter time.

5. *Suppose that Jack, a good friend of yours, became very ill. You advise him to see a doctor right away, but he says that just lately he has had an examination by a good doctor and that it is his practice to undergo a physical examination just once a year. What would you think of him? Which is more dangerous, to be seriously ill in body or in soul? How can one be seriously ill in soul? Do you think it well to remain away from confession after one has sinned seriously? Why not? How soon should one go to confession after one has sinned seriously? What does confession do for the soul?*

If Jack acted in such a way, one would certainly suspect that his mind, as well as his body, was in need of medical attention. Annual care by a physician is a fine thing, but it does not insure perfect health for another whole year; the doctor must of course be again consulted during the year whenever any serious disorders arise.

The health of the body is important only for this life, but the condition of the soul determines our life hereafter; consequently it is much worse to be seriously ill in soul than in body. One is seriously ill in soul when the life of that soul is impaired by mortal sin; in such a condition the union of the soul with God is destroyed because of the loss of sanctifying grace; should death occur at such a time the soul would be excluded from the Beatific Vision.

If a person very ill is foolish not to call a doctor, one in a state of serious sin is much more foolish not to go to confession at once, because he stands in danger of a greater loss, the loss and eternal damnation of his soul. Moreover, the cures of doctors are not always certain, but the curing effect of confession on a person's soul is certain if he is rightly disposed for the reception of the sacrament.

After one has sinned seriously he should go to confession as soon as possible. He should be willing even to undergo some inconvenience in order to restore the life of his soul. Confession not only takes away all mortal sin and the eternal punishment due to sin, but lessens the temporal punishment due to sin and restores sanctifying grace to the soul, thus uniting it to God, restoring its health, and giving it strength for the future.

6. *Mary Webb says she sees no reason why she should go to confession and Holy Communion more than once a year. She never cheats or steals, she does others no wrong and she goes to church every Sunday. What would you tell her?*

Although Mary does nothing seriously wrong now, she has no assurance that she will always continue to live in this manner. She ought to go much oftener to confession to receive the great benefits of that sacrament. It would absolve her from the small sins she does commit, lessen the temporal punishment due to sin, and help her to overcome her faults; more than that, the sacrament of penance increases sanctifying grace in the soul, and gives the soul a right to other graces, thus strengthening it against future dangers that may arise and uniting it more closely to God. Mary ought also to receive the Holy Eucharist as often as possible because our Lord gave that precious sacrament to us as the "Bread of Life," which is as necessary for our souls as material food is for our bodies. Without this wondrous nourishment, the soul fails to grow in sanctity, becomes weak, and lies dangerously exposed to the temptations of Satan. Our Lord said, "He that eateth My Flesh, and drinketh My Blood, hath everlasting life: and I will raise him up in the last day. For My Flesh is meat indeed: and My Blood is drink indeed. He that eateth My Flesh, and drinketh My Blood, abideth in Me, and I in him" (John vi. 55–57). When she has better heeded these words and experienced the joy, consolation, and spiritual strength which flow from the frequent reception of Holy Communion, Mary will better appreciate what one loses in neglecting the frequent use of the Sacraments.

7. *A prominent business man of your parish, Mr. Dean, is refused Catholic burial by the pastor. For what reasons could the pastor refuse Catholic burial to a person? Mary Dean, one of the children of the family, tells you that the whole family is very angry because the pastor refused to bury her father from the Church and that they do not intend to belong to the Catholic Church any longer. Could you say anything to Mary to show her the priest was right? What about the family giving up their religion?*

The pastor could deny Christian burial to a person included in any one of the following categories, unless the person showed signs of repentance before death:

1) Persons publicly known to have denied the truths of the Catholic Faith, to be members of some non-Catholic religious organization, or to be members of a Masonic or other forbidden society.

2) Persons who have been excommunicated from the Church.

3) Those who have deliberately committed suicide.

4) Those killed in a duel.

5) Those who ordered their bodies to be cremated.

6) Those known by the community as great sinners (such as murderers), or those who publicly and obstinately refused the last sacraments when near death.

Mary should be told that the only reasons for denying Catholic burial are very serious ones. Although the priest dislikes to refuse, he is bound by the law of the Church, which, far from being harsh, is most lenient when there are any signs of repentance. But some restriction is necessary because of the wrong ideas and scandal which would arise from giving all the last rites and saying Mass publicly for those who openly and persistently disobeyed the Church. Mr. Dean forced the Church to refuse him Catholic burial when he made himself a member of one of the classes we have enumerated. It is possible, and we may sincerely hope, that Mr. Dean received the grace of repentance at the very last moment, and died reconciled to God. But without signs of such repentance the Church can hardly bring opprobrium upon herself and upon religion in general by publicly officiating at the burial of such a person.

Although the impossibility of their father receiving a Catholic burial is surely a hard thing to bear, it would be most foolish for the Dean family to allow this to unbalance them so completely as to give up their religion. Such an action could not help in any way. It would only further lessen their respect in the eyes of men by marking them as moral cowards and weaklings in their faith. It would add to the first tragedy, the new tragedy of the estrangement from God of every member of the family. It would be more foolish than a child destroying all his toys because his parents were not able to give him one particular toy he desired. A much better procedure on the part of the Dean family would be to continue as members of the Church and offer their fervent prayers for the happy repose of their father's soul.

8. *Mrs. Delaney is supposed to be a Catholic, but you never see her in Church. Later you learn that she goes to Mass and the sacraments in a Catholic church to which she does not belong. Has she a right to go where she pleases? Suppose all the members of a parish did as Mrs. Delaney, what would be the result? May she make her Easter Communion at another church? Ought she to do so? Why?*

Mrs. Delaney has no right at all to go where she pleases to Mass and the sacraments. A pastor is appointed over the souls of his parish to guide them along the highway to God. The word *pastor* or *shepherd* itself implies that all the members of his flock should be led by him and not wander off into other places. One may occasionally go outside his parish to Mass for the sake of convenience, or go to another church for confession, but most of his religious duties should be fulfilled in his own parish church. If all the members of the parish did as Mrs. Delaney, there would arise utter confusion in the parishes concerned. One pastor would be without a flock to care for, while other priests would be overburdened and not able to look after their own parishioners properly.

Mrs. Delaney may make her Easter Communion at another church, but she ought not to do so because it shows little regard for her home parish and gives her pastor no way of knowing whether she has fulfilled her obligation. If she must make her Easter Communion in another parish, she should make the fact known to her pastor to relieve him of doubt in the matter.

9. *James Lane was very ill at Easter time and could not make his Easter duty. He says that he need not receive the sacraments now for another year. Do you agree with him? When should he go to the sacraments?*

James Lane is mistaken in regard to his Easter duty. When one has been unable to receive Holy Eucharist during the proper time, the obligation to do so remains, and the person must fulfill this duty as soon as he can do so. James, then, must receive Holy Communion when he has recovered from his illness.

10. *Mrs. Cade says that she does not think her little girl ought to make her First Holy Communion until she knows what she is about, say at the age of twelve. Mrs. Cade herself was not allowed to go to First Communion until she was that old, and she sees no reason why the Church should have changed her views since. What would you tell her? What does Holy Communion do for the soul? At what age should children go to First Holy Communion? What pope wished to have children receive Holy Communion at an early age? What name has he therefore received?*

The Church has not really changed its views on the reception of Holy Communion by children but has merely returned to the older and correct Catholic concept which for many years was rather obscured, especially in certain parts of the Christian world. The grace received in Holy Communion works upon the soul automatically, as long as there is no obstacle to obstruct it. Consequently the dispositions, knowledge, and amount of preparation of the person receiving Holy Communion are important only as *increasing* grace; they do not *cause* its entrance into the soul. With this view in mind, the Eucharist was for many centuries given to children, sometimes even to very young children, in order that they might not be deprived of its abundant grace. Later on, because of the devastating influence of certain rigorous teachings (Jansenism) which were condemned by the Church, there grew up a tendency to deny Holy Communion to children until they were twelve or fourteen years of age. Extremes of this practice were condemned, but not until the pontificate of Pope Pius X, did children again receive their rightful place at the Eucharistic table. This Pope decreed that children who have reached the age of discretion, commonly about seven years of age, should be allowed to receive Holy Communion after due preparation has been given them. Seven years or thereabouts is, then, the age at which children may and should receive Holy Communion today. Pope Pius X, because of his great desire that all, and especially children, should receive our Lord often in Holy Communion, has been called "The Pope of frequent Communion."

Mrs. Cade should be very glad that her daughter is able to receive the Body and Blood of her Lord at an earlier age than she herself was able to do. The wonderful effects of this Holy Sacrament are imparted to a child's soul even though the child has not as yet acquired a thorough and complete knowledge of all the truths of faith. We should remember the words our Lord once spoke concerning children: "Suffer the little ones to come unto Me."

Holy Communion produces the following effects in the souls of those receiving it worthily:

1) It increases sanctifying grace and the love of God.

2) It takes away venial sins.

3) It helps toward final perseverance by lessening sinful tendencies, preserving from mortal sin, and giving strength in the practice of good works.

11. *James Martin went to confession and Holy Communion on Ash Wednesday. Has he made his Easter duty? During what period of time should he have gone in order to fulfill his obligation?*

No, James Martin has not made his Easter duty, because he received the sacraments before the time for fulfilling this obligation had begun. From the first Sunday in Lent until Trinity Sunday is the time allowed in this country for the making of one's Easter duty. But James received Holy Communion on Ash Wednesday, which occurs several days before the first Sunday in Lent.

12. *John's uncle has just lately come over from Europe. He says in his country Easter time lasts from Palm Sunday to Low Sunday. How can that be? Can you learn more about this for your class?*

In the country from which John's uncle came, as well as in many other countries, the time for fulfilling the Easter duty is from Palm Sunday until Low Sunday, that is, until the first Sunday after Easter. This period is known as the Paschal season and is the time during which Holy Communion must be received according to the general law of the Church. However, Pope Pius VIII granted to American bishops the privilege of extending the period for Easter duty in their dioceses from the first Sunday in Lent to Trinity Sunday. Bishops in other countries, too, may extend the period set by the general Church law; for example, from the fourth Sunday of Lent until Trinity Sunday. So we see that the time allowed for the Easter Communion varies somewhat according to the country in which one lives.

13. *Edna says that she is not good enough to go to Holy Communion often. What would you answer her?*

One should tell Edna that we receive Holy Communion not because we *are* already good, but in order to *become* good. Our Lord did not institute this Holy Sacrament as a reward for perfect souls, but He gives it to all of us as a most nourishing spiritual food that we may grow in perfection. Of course, one whose soul is turned against God by mortal sin cannot receive Holy Communion until he has again received sanctifying grace into his soul by a worthy confession. But one guilty of venial sins alone, may and should receive Holy Communion as often as possible. No one is really worthy of receiving this Holy Sacrament, but one who receives it often will become less and less unworthy.

14. *If a man received Holy Communion unworthily at Easter time, would he have fulfilled the law of the Church?*

It is specifically stated in the Code of the Church's Laws that the Commandment of the Church on receiving Holy Communion during the Easter time is not fulfilled by a sacrilegious or unworthy Communion. It is quite obvious that a person could not fulfill one of his religious obligations by committing a grave sin. If a person attempted to do so, he would commit a mortal sin and would still be obliged to fulfill his Easter duty. He would first have to make a good confession and then receive Holy Communion worthily.

Problem Questions, Chap. XLI, p. 376.

1. *Donald Brunner, twenty-one years of age, has a permanent position, is drawing a good salary, and has no one to support but himself. He feels that he is not obliged to contribute to the church because his parents are regular contributors. Why is Donald obliged to contribute? How could Donald be led to understand his duty?*

Donald Brunner is not a minor; he has reached the age at which he is no longer looked upon as a youth but as a man. Now every honor and every privilege implies corresponding duties. Donald is enjoying manhood and financial independence. His financial obligations, therefore, rest not upon his parents but upon himself. If the government commands that Donald pay taxes, he cannot say that he is not obliged to, just because his parents pay.

He should realize that contributions to the Church as such are not alms. They are merely slight compensations for services rendered. As a member of the Church he is entitled to all of its services and privileges. In accepting these he in a sense binds himself to a contract, which obliges him to make some slight compensation. The Church asks only that its members give in accordance with their means. Donald's position and salary demand that he contribute.

The Church as an organization must have financial support in order that it might the better teach all nations. For this support the Church in the United States relies not upon the government but upon its members. The priests of the Church by their very calling have dedicated their lives to God and service of souls. Due to their state in life they must rely upon the people for their livelihood because "they who preach the gospel, should live by the gospel" (I Cor. ix. 14).

Donald should realize further that he is but the custodian of that which he earns; that all things come from God and thus belong to Him; that in contributing to God's Church he is merely giving back to God more directly that which is truly His.

Problem Questions, Chap. XLI, p. 382.

1. *Jim Michaels and Olive Clancy, second cousins, wish to marry. Jim's mother was a Catholic but Jim was never baptized. Olive insists upon a Catholic marriage. What must be done? Name the various impediments to this union.*

There are two impediments to the marriage of Jim Michaels and Olive Clancy. The first is consanguinity or blood relationship; the second is disparity of worship because the one party is a Catholic and the other is not baptized.

If Jim is baptized and becomes a Catholic, then only one dispensation is necessary, that of consanguinity. Marriages between close relatives are forbidden by the Church because very often children born of such marriages are physically or mentally deficient. If Jim does not become a Catholic the marriage should be discouraged if possible because of the evils often resulting from mixed marriages. If, however, there is a very grave reason for the marriage and both parties still insist, a second dispensation is necessary, that of disparity of worship. This dispensation will be granted only when assurance is given that:

1) The Catholic party will be allowed free exercise of religion.

2) All children will be brought up in the Catholic religion.

3) The non-Catholic party will receive instructions in the Catholic religion, so as to understand its fundamental beliefs, particularly its teaching on marriage as a sacrament and all that doctrine implies.

Marriages with the unbaptized are, as a rule, severely forbidden. There must be grave reasons for contracting such a union; for example, a well-founded hope of conversion of the non-Catholic party after the marriage. The promise mentioned above must be made in writing and signed by both parties. Then and only then may Jim and Olive be married.

2. *Jane Dugan and Frank Sullivan had set their wedding date for March the seventeenth. For some weeks arrangements had been under way. About a month before the ceremony took place, they went to see the pastor about the publication of the banns. They were sorely disappointed when they could not have a nuptial Mass except by special dispensation from the bishop and even then, they could not have a dancing party afterwards. Why does the Church forbid solemnization of marriage during Lent? Does this mean no one can be married during Lent without the bishop's dispensation? Discuss.*

The solemnization of marriage is forbidden during Lent because it is a season of penance and sorrow for sin. It is a season set aside by the Church for meditation on the mystery of the Redemption, and on the Passion and Death of our Lord. It would be unseemly and improper to divert our minds from so solemn a subject by events usually accompanied by worldly festivities.

This, however, does not mean that Catholics cannot be married during Lent without a dispensation from the bishop. They can be married during that time, but the ceremony consists of the marriage proper without Mass, without the solemn nuptial blessing, and without pomp and festivity. With the bishop's dispensation the regular nuptial blessing may, for a just cause, be given during Lent. This dispensation brings with it the permission to have the regular nuptial Mass.

37.

THE SAINTS

Problem Questions, Chap. XLII, p. 390.

1. *What is a saint?*

A saint is one who now enjoys heaven and who died in the state of sanctifying grace. He (or she) need not be canonized to be a saint, but most often when we speak of a saint we mean someone canonized by the Church. Sometimes we call living people "saints" because they are like the saints in holiness.

(Reference: *The Catechism Explained*, Spirago-Clarke.)

2. Name your patron saints. What is his (her) feast day?

---

3. Write a biography of a saint you like.

One of the favorite saints of today is the childlike Teresa of Lisieux who is best known in America as the "Little Flower." Before she became a nun her name was Mary Frances Teresa Martin. "Little Teresa" was born during the lifetime of many people who are living today. In fact, four of her sisters are still alive. The Saint was born at Alençon, France, on January 2, 1873. Before she was five years old her mother died. To her good father and older sisters was left the duty of raising her. With such a group caring for her she grew as the Christ Child in wisdom and grace. At the age of fifteen "Little Teresa," by special permission, became Sister Teresa of the Child Jesus in the Carmelite convent at Lisieux. Her sisters Marie, Celine, and Pauline also became Carmelite nuns while Leonie became a Visitandine. Sister Teresa by the grace of God perfected her life during her nine years as a Carmelite. She used as a means of perfecting herself a way which is today known by the name she gave it, the "little way" of St. Teresa. It is the way of confidence and love, "the way of spiritual childhood, the way of trust and absolute self-surrender." The Little Flower did not do great things as some saints have, but following her "little way" she made things great by doing them for the love of God. On September 30, 1897, after nearly six months of suffering, she died. Since then she has fulfilled her promise of "letting fall a shower of roses" to such an extent that Pope Pius XI has called her a "prodigy of miracles." Teresa the "miracle of virtues" and "prodigy of miracles" and most beloved saint of the age was canonized on May 17, 1925. Her feast day is celebrated every year on the day of her death and birth into heaven.

(Reference: *A Little White Flower, the Autobiography of St. Thérèse of Lisieux.*)

4. Are there any saints today?

It is probable that there are people alive today who will be canonized saints at some time in the future.

5. Were there any saints in the nineteenth century?

There were a number of saints in the nineteenth century. The Curé d'Ars (St. John Vianney) and St. Teresa are the two most outstanding ones. Then there is St. Bernadette of Lourdes, St. Gabriel Possenti, and others.

6. Are there any American saints?

The saints known as the Jesuit martyrs are American saints. They are Father Isaac Jogues, Brother Rene Goupil, and John of La Lande, an Oblate, who were martyred by the Indians in what is now part of the United States. Father John de Brébeuf, Gabriel Lalemand, Charles Garnier, and Noel Chabonel died for the Faith in Canada. St. Rose of Lima is a South American saint.

(Reference: *Saint Andrew's Daily Missal.*)

7. Read the Litany of the Saints. Are the lives of the saints any evidence of the holiness of the Church?

The lives of the saints are an evidence of the holiness of the Church. One cannot conceive of the Mother of such a multitude of holy souls in every succeeding century since the time of Christ as otherwise than holy. Could she who taught an Augustine, a Francis of Assisi or of Sales, a Thomas, a Catherine, a Teresa, a "Little Teresa," a John Vianney, saints whose virtues have surpassed anything human nature alone can produce, could the Church have taught these saints their holiness without herself possessing a superabundance of that very quality?

8. What is meant by beatification?

Beatification is a papal decree giving permission to venerate a martyr, or a soul whose extraordinary holiness is evident from examination and is vouched for by proved miracles. This permission extends usually to a specified territory and only to certain liturgical exercises. It is not an infallible decree because it merely allows veneration. One who has been "beatified" is called "blessed."

(Reference: Article "Beatification" in the *Catholic Encyclopedia.*)

9. *What is meant by canonization?*

Canonization is an infallible decree of the pope commanding veneration of a (beatified) martyr, or of a soul whose extraordinary holiness is evident from repeated examinations and is vouched for by proved miracles which have occurred since his (or her) beatification.

Here are the words of canonization; — "In honor of .... we decree, define, and inscribe in the catalog of the saints that Blessed .... is a saint, and we order that each year on ...., his feast day, his memory be recalled with affectionate devotion by the Universal Church."

We must remember that these decrees do not place a person in heaven, but declare that a person is in heaven and should be honored by the Church.

10. *What honor and devotion is shown to saints?*

We honor the saints in the liturgy of the Church, that is, in the Mass and the Divine Office. We venerate the saints in various devotional exercises as, for instance, by saying the litany of the saints, by praying to them, and by honoring their relics and images. This honor is known as the worship of "dulia" which is honor given to the saints because of the supernatural graces and gifts which they have received from God.

11. *Discuss the honor and devotion to the saints in the light of the first commandment of God.*

There are many who believe that it is a sin against the first commandment to honor the saints. It is not. The saints are not "strange gods." They are the favorite children of our Heavenly Father. When we honor a child we thereby honor his parents. The saints are the masterpieces of the greatest Artist. When we praise or treasure or honor a masterpiece we honor the artist. The saints are the very creation of God and therefore belong to Him. Thus when we honor them we do nothing else than worship God in the saints. When we venerate the saints we at the same time worship the Father, the greatest of artists, the Creator. In the words of the definition of the worship of "dulia" we honor the saints because of the supernatural graces and gifts that they have received from God. Hence we must conclude that since we honor the saints because of God, and since in honoring the saints we honor God, the veneration of the saints is entirely legitimate and commendable.

12. *Are the saints (as used in this chapter) the only members of the Church Triumphant?*
All those who are enjoying the gift of eternal happiness are the members of the Church Triumphant.

13. *Are there any uncanonized saints?*
It is safe to say that many saints have not been canonized.

14. *Why is the communion of saints a consoling doctrine?*
The communion of saints is a consoling doctrine because we can help one another in this life by our prayers and good works, we can help the souls in purgatory, we can expect the help of others when we are in purgatory, and finally because we can appeal to the powerful intercession of the saints.

15. *How may the Church Militant help the Church Suffering?*
The prayers and good works of the Church Militant help the Church Suffering by satisfying for part of the punishment the poor souls must undergo before they can enter heaven.

16. *How may the Church Triumphant help the Church Suffering and the Church Militant?*
The Church Triumphant helps the Church Suffering and the Church Militant by its powerful intercession.

17. *Why may we pray to the saints?*
We may pray to the saints because by doing so we honor God, the Author of all grace. Since the saints are our brothers and at the same time favorite children of God, we may legitimately ask for and expect their help.

18. *How does this differ from prayers to God?*

Prayers are offered to God because of His own supreme excellence. They are addressed directly to Him. Prayers are offered to the saints because of the gifts they have received from God. Prayers to the saints are honor paid to God in the saints, or are a petition for the intercession of the saints.

38.

THE ANGELS

Problem Questions, Chap. XLIII, p. 397.

1. *Make a list of the appearances of angels in connection with the life of Christ.*

"The Angel Gabriel was sent from God into a city of Galilee called Nazareth" to announce to the Blessed Virgin that she was to be the Mother of God (Luke i. 26).

The angel of the Lord stood by the shepherds in the field bringing them the good tidings of great joy: "For this day is born to you a Savior, who is Christ the Lord, in the city of David" (Luke ii. 11).

The angel of the Lord appeared to Joseph in his sleep and said: "Joseph, son of David, fear not to take unto thee Mary thy wife, for that which is conceived in her is of the Holy Ghost. And she shall bring forth a Son; and thou shalt call His name Jesus. For He shall save His people from their sins" (Matt. i. 20–21).

The angel of the Lord appeared again to Joseph in his sleep, commanding him to take the child and his mother, and fly into Egypt — "Herod will seek the Child to destroy Him" (Matt. ii. 13).

Upon Herod's death, an angel of the Lord appeared to Joseph in his sleep, to tell him that it was safe to bring back to Israel the mother and the Child (Matt. ii. 20).

After Christ was tempted in the desert, angels came and ministered unto Him (Matt. iv. 11).

In the Garden of Gethsemane an angel appeared to Christ, strengthening Him (Luke xxii. 43).

An angel appeared to the women who came to the sepulcher to anoint Christ, and said to them: "Fear not you; for I know that you seek Jesus who was crucified" (Matt. xxviii. 5).

Two angels appeared to Mary Magdalen in the sepulcher where Jesus had been laid (John xx. 12).

At the Ascension of Jesus into heaven, two angels appeared to the disciples (Acts i. 10).

2. *Make a list of some of the appearances of angels in the Old·Testament. (A concordance might be used to answer this question completely.)*

God placed before the paradise of pleasure cherubims (Gen. iii. 24). An angel appeared to Agar, the handmaid of Sarah, the wife of Abraham, when Agar fled into the desert. The angel told Agar to return to Sarah, and revealed to her the future life of her son Ismael (Gen. xvi. 1–3).

Angels visited Abraham and were entertained by him. They foretold the birth of his son Isaac (Gen. xviii. 22).

Two angels visited Lot at his home in the doomed city of Sodom and rescued him with his family from the general conflagration (Gen. xix. 1 *sq.*).

An angel visited Abraham to prevent him from offering his son Isaac as a sacrifice to God (Gen. xxii. 10–12).

Angels met Jacob in his journey; and later, one wrestled with him and blessed him and changed his name to Israel (Gen. xxxii. 1; 24 *sq.*).

An angel appeared to Balaam and stopped him from going to curse Israel (Num. xxii. 22).

An angel fed Elias in the desert (III Kings xix. 5).

An angel accompanied Tobias on a long journey, doing him many services, and at length manifested his real personality. saying: "I am the angel Raphael, one of the seven who stand before the throne of the Lord" (Tob. xii. 15).

An angel shielded from harm the three saintly youths in the fiery furnace (Dan. iii. 49).

The angel Gabriel visited Daniel to reveal to him the wondrous prophecy of the seventy weeks to the coming of the Messiah (Dan. ix. 21 *sq.*).

3. *What were the names of angels who have appeared to men?*
Only three of the highest angels are mentioned in the Sacred Scriptures by name:
Michael (who is like to God) (Jude i. 9).
Gabriel (man of God) (Luke i. 26).
Raphael (God heals) (Tob. xii. 15).

4. *What did Christ say regarding our guardian angels?*
Christ shows that the little ones on earth are not to be offended or despised, because they are so dear in the sight of God, as to have in His presence their angels who protect them. "Take heed that you despise not one of these little ones; for I say to you that their angels in heaven always see the face of My Father who is in heaven" (Matt. xvii. 10).

5. *In what ways does the guardian angel look after us?*
The chief purpose of the activity of our guardian angels is our spiritual good. As the one thing necessary in this life of probation is to know, love, and serve God, and thus to reach supreme happiness in heaven, their main object is to assist us to the attainment of this one purpose in life. As faithful mentors, they, on the one hand, flash upon our minds rays of heavenly light, by which our understanding is illumined with the knowledge of God and eternal truths, and inspired with good thoughts that aid us to advance in the paths of virtue; and on the other hand, they incline indirectly our wills to good works, instill into our hearts salutary emotions, enkindle heavenly desires, inflame our love for God and our neighbors, remove present obstacles, as well as occasions of sin, and by interior warnings encourage us to overcome evil.
While aiding us in the spiritual life, guardian angels are not oblivious of our material good. Taking charge of us from our birth, they exercise particular care for us as infants, and protect

us from the many dangers to which childhood is exposed. As we advance in years they do not abandon us, but remain always at our side and death alone ends their watchfulness over our physical welfare.

The guardian angels assist us to overcome the power of the evil powers and hold them in check. They also offer to God the prayers and good works of their clients. They make constant intercession for us, and while bearing our prayers on high, they also make them more acceptable to God, by uniting their own ardent prayers with ours.

6. *Why do you think that at certain times hosts or multitudes of angels appear? Why would a multitude more fully express praise of God?*

The angels appeared at Christ's birth under the form of a "heavenly army" (Luke ii. 13), in order to indicate to men their large number, their hierarchy, and their power. The divinity of Christ seemed hidden beneath His flesh; it was obscured, as it were, by the swaddling clothes, manger, and later by the temptation of Satan (Matt. iv. 2). At the same time, the appearance of the angelic army at His birth, the advent of many angels to serve Him after the temptation, clearly show that He was God.

The fact that a multitude of angels praises God shows how inexhaustible are God's perfections and glory.

7. *What is the basis for representing angels with wings? Have any angels wings? Have all angels wings?*

Angels are usually represented as winged adolescents. Youth is a symbol of strength and grace. The wings are symbols of the angels' spirituality, immortality, and office as messengers of God. The bodily element in representations of angels is as subdued and as ethereal as possible in order to convey the idea that angels are pure spirits. The eyes and the face of the angels — when the representation is a work of art — express the angels' intelligence and superior knowledge.

The angels are pure spirits, and hence do not possess either bodies or wings.

8. *Select two pictures of angels that you like. Tell why.*
The Nativity, Giotto.
The Annunciation, Fra Angelico.
The Nativity, Botticelli.
Tobias and the Angel, Savoldo.
(Cf. *The Gospel Story in Art,* by John La Farge.)

9. *Why is the "Angelus" called by that name?*
The Angelus, a devotion in honor of the Incarnation of our Lord and venerating His Blessed Mother, takes its name from the opening word of the Latin form: *Angelus Domini nuntiavit Mariae* (The Angel of the Lord declared unto Mary).

10. *Find a poem on an angel that you like. Memorize it. What is its fundamental idea?*
From "Lead Kindly Light," by Cardinal Newman.

> My oldest friend, mine from the hour
>   When first I drew my breath;
> My faithful friend, that shall be mine
>   Unfailing till my death.
>
> No Patron Saint, nor Mary's love,
>   The dearest and the best,
> Has known my being, as thou hast known,
>   And blest as thou hast blest.
>
> Thou wast my sponsor at the font,
>   And thou, each budding year,
> Didst whisper elements of truth,
>   Into my childish ear.
>
> And thou wilt linger round my bed,
>   When life is ebbing low;
> Of doubt, impatience, and of gloom
>   The jealous sleepless foe.
>
> And mine, O Brother of my soul,
>   When my release shall come;
> Thy gentle arms shall lift me then,
>   Thy wings shall waft me home.

39.

THE END OF THE JOURNEY

Problem Questions, Chap. XLIV, p. 405.

1. *Where are you going?*

I hope to go to heaven when I die. God placed me in this world to know Him, to love Him, and to serve Him, and thus to merit heaven. In heaven I will enjoy the happiness which I have longed for throughout my life. I may seek riches, place, pleasures, and knowledge, but not one of these will completely satisfy me. The longer I live the more I realize the truth of St. Augustine's words: "Thou hast made us for Thyself, O God, and our hearts are not at rest until they rest in Thee." To gain this happiness, I must first know God. I will love Him if I really know Him. If I love Him, I will do all He wishes me to do and hence merit heaven.

2. *What is heaven?*

Heaven is a state of perfect and everlasting happiness for the angels and the saints. It is also a place where dwell the risen Christ, the Blessed Virgin, and the other heavenly inhabitants. There the souls of the just enjoy the Beatific Vision forever and with it all good things. The Blessed in heaven are free from all evils. They shall neither hunger nor thirst (Apoc. vii. 16); death shall be no more, nor mourning (Apoc. xxi. 4) and night will be no more (Apoc. xxii. 5).

3. *What is hell?*

Hell is at once a state of punishment for those who die in mortal sin and the place where they are held. There the condemned souls will suffer for all eternity the pain of loss and the pain of sense. The pain of loss is a perpetual privation of the Beatific Vision and of all the blessings which flow therefrom, namely, companionship with Christ, the Blessed Virgin, the angels, and the saints.

The pain of sense is the pain caused by an external sensible medium, which will in some way effect the damned souls and also the risen body after the final resurrection. Sacred Scripture describes hell as a prison, a place of darkness, of weeping and of gnashing of teeth, and as a pool of fire and brimstone. From these expressions we can conclude that the lot of the damned is very pitiful indeed.

Hell's fire is a real fire torturing — yet never consuming — those who are lost.

4. What is purgatory?

Purgatory is a state of temporary punishment for those who, departing this life in the grace of God, are not entirely free from venial sins or have not yet fully paid the debt of temporal punishment due to their sins.

5. What is the Particular Judgment?

Immediately after death God judges each individual soul and rewards or punishes it according to its deeds. At the particular judgment the eternal lot of every soul is decided by the just judgment of God.

6. What is the General Judgment?

The final resurrection will be followed by the general judgment in which everyone will give an account of his works. The sentence will be pronounced by Christ as Man. It is becoming that He who merited eternal life for us should Himself usher us into it. His glorious coming will be accompanied by a sign in the heavens, which according to Tradition and Liturgy will be a cross. The twelve Apostles will ratify the sentence of Christ, the Judge. The final judgment will make known the hidden ways of God, and manifest the majesty of Christ, the glory of the just, and the confusion of the sinners.

7. What judgment is expressed in the examination of conscience?

The particular examination of conscience suggests the particular judgment; the general examination of conscience suggests the general judgment.

*8. What is meant by the resurrection of the body? What ref-
erence is there to this doctrine in the Old Testament? What is
the basis of our belief in this doctrine?*

It is of faith that at the end of time, all men will rise in the
bodies they now possess. Old Testament references to the doctrine of the resurrection of the body are: Job xix. 23–26; Isaias
xxvi. 19; Daniel xii. 2; II Machabees vii. 14.

Sacred Scripture, especially the New Testament, clearly pro-
claims the doctrine of the resurrection of the body. Tradition
teaches it as one of the fundamental truths of the Christian
religion.

*9. Will we all be judged alike? or will our capacity and our op-
portunity be taken into account?*

God will judge each man only insofar as he is responsible
for his actions. A man whose mind is darkened by ignorance and
error, whose will is weak and unsteady, is not responsible for his
shortcomings in the same degree as a man whose mind is keen
and well disciplined, whose will is trained and strong. Man is
responsible before the judgment seat of God only to the extent
that he knew what he was doing and freely chose to do it.

10. Are there any clear descriptions of heaven?

There is no complete description of heaven. The clearest description in Sacred Scripture is found in St. Paul's first Epistle
to the Corinthians xiii. 12: "We see now through a glass in a
dark manner; but then face to face. Now I know in part; but
then I shall know even as I am known."

11. What is the Beatific Vision?

The Beatific Vision is a clear and immediate, though not comprehensive, knowledge of God as He is in Himself.

"Clear" — free from all obscurity.

"Immediate" — directly, without the intervention of anything.

"Not comprehensive" — God alone can fully understand Himself.

The threefold knowledge of God by reason, faith, and the

Beatific Vision may be compared to the knowledge which I have of a painter. I may know the painter mediately through his productions, or secondly, I may come to know him through the testimony of someone who saw him, thirdly, I may know him by direct vision.

12. *Comment on the thirteenth chapter of the First Epistle to the Corinthians in the light of this chapter.*

I Corinthians xiii. 12. "We see now through a glass in a dark manner: but then face to face. Now I know in part; but then I shall know even as I am known." In this life we have no direct knowledge of God. We see Him only indirectly, much the same as we see an object reflected "in a mirror." As we see only the reflection, and see it in an imperfect medium, we see God imperfectly, indistinctly. Our reason can learn something of God and of His attributes from the "things that are made" (Rom. i. 20). Revelation adds to our knowledge; but, it is likewise indirect and incomplete.

In heaven we shall know and see God face to face, that is, directly and completely, as He knows us.

www.ingramcontent.com/pod-product-compliance
Lightning Source LLC
LaVergne TN
LVHW051515080426
835509LV00017B/2072